American Literature Teacher's Guide

CONTENTS

Editor: Alan Christopherson, M.S.

Alpha Omega Publications®

804 N. 2nd Ave. E., Rock Rapids, IA 51246-1759
© MM by Alpha Omega Publications, Inc.   All rights reserved.
LIFEPAC is a registered trademark of Alpha Omega Publications, Inc.

OVERVIEW

American Literature

Curriculum Overview
Elective

OBJECTIVES

1. The student will gain a general overview of the development of American literature and thought from Puritanism to Postmodernism.

2. The student will learn to critique the philosophy of each author from a Christian perspective.

3. The student will become aware of the philosophies and religious beliefs that influenced the authors in each period of history.

4. The student will gain knowledge of the historical and biographical background for each author and period.

5. The student will appreciate literature as a reflection of the thought and life of the times.

American Literature Curriculum Overview

American Literature LIFEPAC I	American Literature LIFEPAC 2

Early American Literature 1600–1800

INTRODUCTION

The Puritans

John Smith
William Bradford
John Winthrop

The Colonists

Mary Rowlandson
Anne Bradstreet
Edward Taylor
Samuel Sewall

The Days of Change and Revolution 1700–1800

Jonathan Edwards
Benjamin Franklin
Thomas Paine
Thomas Jefferson
Michel-Guillaume Jean de Crèvecoeur

Romantic Period

A NEW NATION 1800–1840

INTRODUCTION

Washington Irving
James Fenimore Cooper
William Cullen Bryant

American Renaissance 1840–1855

INTRODUCTION

THE FIRESIDE POETS

Henry Wadsworth Longfellow
John Greenleaf Whittier
Oliver Wendell Holmes

THE TRANSCENDENTALISTS

Ralph Waldo Emerson
Henry David Thoreau
Walt Whitman

Poets of Despair

Edgar Allen Poe
Nathaniel Hawthorne
Herman Melville
Emily Dickinson

American Literature LIFEPAC 3	American Literature LIFEPAC 4

War and Reconciliation 1855–1865

SECESSION AND LOYALTY

INTRODUCTION

Frederick Douglas
Harriet Beecher Stowe
Spirituals
Robert E. Lee
Abraham Lincoln

Realism and Naturalism 1865–1915

INTRODUCTION

Samuel Langhorne Clemens
William Dean Howells
Henry James

Naturalists, Regionalists, and Realists

Stephen Crane
Kate Chopin
Paul Laurence Dunbar
Jack London

The Modern Age 1915–1946

MODERN PROSE

Ernest Hemingway
F. Scott Fitzgerald

Modern Poetry

Ezra Pound
Carl Sandburg
E.E. Cummings
Wallace Stevens
Robert Frost
W.H. Auden

Other Modern Age Literature

Harlem Renaissance — Langston Hughes

Drama — Thornton Wilder

Religious Works — J. Grescham Machen

American Literature LIFEPAC 5

**From Modern to Postmodern
1946–Present**

INTRODUCTION

Flannery O'Connor
Theodore Roethke

More Contemporary Writers

Eudora Welty
John Updike
Robert Trail Spence Lowell, Jr.

Social issues

Martin Luther King, Jr.
Ralph Ellison
Gwendolyn Brooks

MANAGEMENT

STRUCTURE OF THE LIFEPAC CURRICULUM

The LIFEPAC curriculum is conveniently structured to provide one teacher handbook containing teacher support material with answer keys and ten student worktexts for each subject at grade levels two through twelve. The worktext format of the LIFEPACs allows the student to read the textual information and complete workbook activities all in the same booklet. The easy to follow LIFEPAC numbering system lists the grade as the first number(s) and the last two digits as the number of the series. For example, the Language Arts LIFEPAC at the 6th grade level, 5th book in the series would be LAN0605.

Each LIFEPAC is divided into 3 to 5 sections and begins with an introduction or overview of the booklet as well as a series of specific learning objectives to give a purpose to the study of the LIFEPAC. The introduction and objectives are followed by a vocabulary section which may be found at the beginning of each section at the lower levels, at the beginning of the LIFEPAC in the middle grades, or in the glossary at the high school level. Vocabulary words are used to develop word recognition and should not be confused with the spelling words introduced later in the LIFEPAC. The student should learn all vocabulary words before working the LIFEPAC sections to improve comprehension, retention, and reading skills.

Each activity or written assignment has a number for easy identification, such as 1.1. The first number corresponds to the LIFEPAC section and the number to the right of the decimal is the number of the activity.

Teacher checkpoints, which are essential to maintain quality learning, are found at various locations throughout the LIFEPAC. The teacher should check 1) neatness of work and penmanship, 2) quality of understanding (tested with a short oral quiz), 3) thoroughness of answers (complete sentences and paragraphs, correct spelling, etc.), 4) completion of activities (no blank spaces), and 5) accuracy of answers as compared to the answer key (all answers correct).

The self test questions are also number coded for easy reference. For example, 2.015 means that this is the 15th question in the self test of Section II. The first number corresponds to the LIFEPAC section, the zero indicates that it is a self test question, and the number to the right of the zero the question number.

The LIFEPAC test is packaged at the centerfold of each LIFEPAC. It should be removed and put aside before giving the booklet to the student for study.

Answer and test keys have the same numbering system as the LIFEPACs and appear at the back of this handbook. The student may be given access to the answer keys (not the test keys) under teacher supervision so that they can score their own work.

A thorough study of the Curriculum Overview by the teacher before instruction begins is essential to the success of the student. The teacher should become familiar with expected skill mastery and understand how these grade level skills fit into the overall skill development of the curriculum. The teacher should also preview the objectives that appear at the beginning of each LIFEPAC for additional preparation and planning.

TEST SCORING and GRADING

Answer keys and test keys give examples of correct answers. They convey the idea, but the student may use many ways to express a correct answer. The teacher should check for the essence of the answer, not for the exact wording. Many questions are high level and require thinking and creativity on the part of the student. Each answer should be scored based on whether or not the main idea written by the student matches the model example. "Any Order" or "Either Order" in a key indicates that no particular order is necessary to be correct.

Most self tests and LIFEPAC tests at the lower elementary levels are scored at 1 point per question; however, the upper levels may have a point system awarding 2 to 5 points for various questions. Further, the total test points will vary; they may not always equal 100 points. They may be 78, 85, 100, 105, etc.

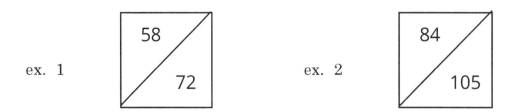

A score box similar to ex.1 above is located at the end of each self test and on the front of the LIFEPAC test. The bottom score, 72, represents the total number of points possible on the test. The upper score, 58, represents the number of points your student will need to receive an 80% or passing grade. If you wish to establish the exact percentage that your student has achieved, find the total points of their correct answers and divide it by the bottom number (in this case 72.) For example, if your student has a point total of 65, divide 65 by 72 for a grade of 90%. Referring to ex. 2, on a test with a total of 105 possible points, the student would have to receive a minimum of 84 correct points for an 80% or passing grade. If your student has received 93 points, simply divide the 93 by 105 for a percentage grade of 89%. Students who receive a score below 80% should review the LIFEPAC and retest using the appropriate Alternate Test found in the Teacher's Guide.

The following is a guideline to assign letter grades for completed LIFEPACs based on a maximum total score of 100 points.

LIFEPAC Test = 60% of the Total Score (or percent grade)

Self Test = 25% of the Total Score (average percent of self tests)

Reports = 10% or 10* points per LIFEPAC

Oral Work = 5% or 5* points per LIFEPAC

*Determined by the teacher's subjective evaluation of the student's daily work.

Example:

LIFEPAC Test Score	=	92%	92	x	.60	=	55 points
Self Test Average	=	90%	90	x	.25	=	23 points
Reports						=	8 points
Oral Work						=	4 points

TOTAL POINTS   =   90 points

Grade Scale based on point system:

100	–	94	=	A
93	–	86	=	B
85	–	77	=	C
76	–	70	=	D
Below		70	=	F

TEACHER HINTS and STUDYING TECHNIQUES

LIFEPAC Activities are written to check the level of understanding of the preceding text. The student may look back to the text as necessary to complete these activities; however, a student should never attempt to do the activities without reading (studying) the text first. Self tests and LIFEPAC tests are never open book tests.

Language arts activities (skill integration) often appear within other subject curriculum. The purpose is to give the student an opportunity to test their skill mastery outside of the context in which it was presented.

Writing complete answers (paragraphs) to some questions is an integral part of the LIFEPAC Curriculum in all subjects. This builds communication and organization skills, increases understanding and retention of ideas, and helps enforce good penmanship. Complete sentences should be encouraged for this type of activity. Obviously, single words or phrases do not meet the intent of the activity, since multiple lines are given for the response.

Review is essential to student success. Time invested in review where review is suggested will be time saved in correcting errors later. Self tests, unlike the section activities, are closed book. This procedure helps to identify weaknesses before they become too great to overcome. Certain objectives from self tests are cumulative and test previous sections; therefore, good preparation for a self test must include all material studied up to that testing point.

The following procedure checklist has been found to be successful in developing good study habits in the LIFEPAC curriculum.

1. Read the introduction and Table of Contents.
2. Read the objectives.
3. Recite and study the entire vocabulary (glossary) list.
4. Study each section as follows:
    a. Read the introduction and study the section objectives.
    b. Read all the text for the entire section, but answer none of the activities.
    c. Return to the beginning of the section and memorize each vocabulary word and definition.
    d. Reread the section, complete the activities, check the answers with the answer key, correct all errors, and have the teacher check.
    e. Read the self test but do not answer the questions.
    f. Go to the beginning of the first section and reread the text and answers to the activities up to the self test you have not yet done.
    g. Answer the questions to the self test without looking back.
    h. Have the self test checked by the teacher.
    i. Correct the self test and have the teacher check the corrections.
    j. Repeat steps a–i for each section.

5. Use the SQ3R* method to prepare for the LIFEPAC test.

> **S**can the whole LIFEPAC.
> **Q**uestion yourself on the objectives.
> **R**ead the whole LIFEPAC again.
> **R**ecite through an oral examination.
> **R**eview weak areas.

6. Take the LIFEPAC test as a closed book test.
7. LIFEPAC tests are administered and scored under direct teacher supervision. Students who receive scores below 80% should review the LIFEPAC using the study method and take the Alternate Test located in the Teacher Handbook. The final test grade may be the grade on the Alternate Test or an average of the grades from the original LIFEPAC test and the Alternate Test.

GOAL SETTING and SCHEDULES

Each school must develop its own schedule, because no single set of procedures will fit every situation. The following is an example of a daily schedule that includes the five LIFEPAC subjects as well as time slotted for special activities.

Possible Daily Schedule

8:15	–	8:25	Pledges, prayer, songs, devotions, etc.
8:25	–	9:10	Bible
9:10	–	9:55	Language Arts
9:55	–	10:15	Recess (juice break)
10:15	–	11:00	Mathematics
11:00	–	11:45	History & Geography
11:45	–	12:30	Lunch, recess, quiet time
12:30	–	1:15	Science
1:15	–		Drill, remedial work, enrichment*

*Enrichment: Computer time, physical education, field trips, fun reading, games and puzzles, family business, hobbies, resource persons, guests, crafts, creative work, electives, music appreciation, projects.

Basically, two factors need to be considered when assigning work to a student in the LIFEPAC curriculum.

The first is time. An average of 45 minutes should be devoted to each subject, each day. Remember, this is only an average. Because of extenuating circumstances a student may spend only 15 minutes on a subject one day and the next day spend 90 minutes on the same subject.

The second factor is the number of pages to be worked in each subject. A single LIFEPAC is designed to take 3 to 4 weeks to complete. Allowing about 3-4 days for LIFEPAC introduction, review, and tests, the student has approximately 15 days to complete the LIFEPAC pages. Simply take the number of pages in the LIFEPAC, divide it by 15 and you will have the number of pages that must be completed on a daily basis to keep the student on schedule. For example, a LIFEPAC containing 45 pages will require 3 completed pages per day. Again, this is only an average. While working a 45 page LIFEPAC, the student may complete only 1 page the first day if the text has a lot of activities or reports, but go on to complete 5 pages the next day.

Long range planning requires some organization. Because the traditional school year originates in the early fall of one year and continues to late spring of the following year, a calendar should be devised that covers this period of time. Approximate beginning and completion dates can be noted on the calendar as well as special occasions such as holidays, vacations and birthdays. Since each LIFEPAC takes 3-4 weeks or eighteen days to complete, it should take about 180 school days to finish a set of ten LIFEPACs. Starting at the beginning school date, mark off eighteen school days on the calendar and that will become the targeted completion date for the first LIFEPAC. Continue marking the calendar until you have established dates for the remaining nine LIFEPACs making adjustments for previously noted holidays and vacations. If all five subjects are being used, the ten established target dates should be the same for the LIFEPACs in each subject.

FORMS

The sample weekly lesson plan and student grading sheet forms are included in this section as teacher support materials and may be duplicated at the convenience of the teacher.

The student grading sheet is provided for those who desire to follow the suggested guidelines for assignment of letter grades found on page 3 of this section. The student's self test scores should be posted as percentage grades. When the LIFEPAC is completed the teacher should average the self test grades, multiply the average by .25 and post the points in the box marked self test points. The LIFEPAC percentage grade should be multiplied by .60 and posted. Next, the teacher should award and post points for written reports and oral work. A report may be any type of written work assigned to the student whether it is a LIFEPAC or additional learning activity. Oral work includes the student's ability to respond orally to questions which may or may not be related to LIFEPAC activities or any type of oral report assigned by the teacher. The points may then be totaled and a final grade entered along with the date that the LIFEPAC was completed.

The Student Record Book which was specifically designed for use with the Alpha Omega curriculum provides space to record weekly progress for one student over a nine week period as well as a place to post self test and LIFEPAC scores. The Student Record Books are available through the current Alpha Omega catalog; however, unlike the enclosed forms these books are not for duplication and should be purchased in sets of four to cover a full academic year.

WEEKLY LESSON PLANNER

Week of:

	Subject	Subject	Subject	Subject
Monday				
	Subject	Subject	Subject	Subject
Tuesday				
	Subject	Subject	Subject	Subject
Wednesday				
	Subject	Subject	Subject	Subject
Thursday				
	Subject	Subject	Subject	Subject
Friday				

WEEKLY LESSON PLANNER

Week of:

	Subject	Subject	Subject	Subject
Monday				
	Subject	Subject	Subject	Subject
Tuesday				
	Subject	Subject	Subject	Subject
Wednesday				
	Subject	Subject	Subject	Subject
Thursday				
	Subject	Subject	Subject	Subject
Friday				

Student Name _____   Year _____

Bible

LP #	Self Test Scores by Sections 1	2	3	4	5	Self Test Points	LIFEPAC Test	Oral Points	Report Points	Final Grade	Date
01											
02											
03											
04											
05											
06											
07											
08											
09											
10											

History & Geography

LP #	Self Test Scores by Sections 1	2	3	4	5	Self Test Points	LIFEPAC Test	Oral Points	Report Points	Final Grade	Date
01											
02											
03											
04											
05											
06											
07											
08											
09											
10											

Language Arts

LP #	Self Test Scores by Sections 1	2	3	4	5	Self Test Points	LIFEPAC Test	Oral Points	Report Points	Final Grade	Date
01											
02											
03											
04											
05											
06											
07											
08											
09											
10											

Student Name _____   Year _____

Mathematics

LP #	Self Test Scores by Sections 1	2	3	4	5	Self Test Points	LIFEPAC Test	Oral Points	Report Points	Final Grade	Date
01											
02											
03											
04											
05											
06											
07											
08											
09											
10											

Science

LP #	Self Test Scores by Sections 1	2	3	4	5	Self Test Points	LIFEPAC Test	Oral Points	Report Points	Final Grade	Date
01											
02											
03											
04											
05											
06											
07											
08											
09											
10											

Spelling/Electives

LP #	Self Test Scores by Sections 1	2	3	4	5	Self Test Points	LIFEPAC Test	Oral Points	Report Points	Final Grade	Date
01											
02											
03											
04											
05											
06											
07											
08											
09											
10											

TEACHER

N
O
T
E
S

23

INSTRUCTIONS FOR AMERICAN LITERATURE

The LIFEPAC curriculum from grades two through twelve is structured so that the daily instructional material is written directly into the LIFEPACs. The student is encouraged to read and follow this instructional material in order to develop independent study habits. The teacher should introduce the LIFEPAC to the student, set a required completion schedule, complete teacher checks, be available for questions regarding both content and procedures, administer and grade tests, and develop additional learning activities as desired. Teachers working with several students may schedule their time so that students are assigned to a quiet work activity when it is necessary to spend instructional time with one particular student.

This course is one in a two-part literature series for high school students. The series complements AOP's current Language Arts program, adding a richness that can only be found in the great books of Western Civilization. The series is designed to enlarge the Christian's understanding of the development of Western Civilization while strengthening him or her in the faith. Its content and methodology utilize the principles of classical education. If applied properly, the inquisitive high school student can benefit greatly from a thorough analysis of the literature that has shaped Western Civilization.

The exercises presented in this course follow a path similar to the classical learning structure: grammar, logic, and rhetoric. Grammar is the basic facts or principles of a subject. Logic (or dialectic) is an understanding of how the facts relate to one another. Rhetoric is the ability to articulate and apply knowledge and understanding with eloquence and wisdom. A parallel structure can be found in Scripture: knowledge (Proverbs 1:7), understanding (Job 28:28), and wisdom (Eccl. 12:9).

The student is required to master the "grammar" of the course by completing short answer questions dispersed throughout the text. Their knowledge of the course's "grammar" will be checked on Self-Tests and Tests.

A logically understanding of the facts are encouraged through the "What to Look For" and "For Thought and Discussion" exercises. "What to Look For" exercises are included before certain readings. This encourages attentive reading and will prepare the student for the corresponding "For Thought and Discussion" exercises. "For Thought and Discussion" exercises are included at the end of each Self-Test. They are meant to facilitate discussion between the student and the teacher on a specific subject for the means of developing a more thoroughly Christian worldview. A Scriptural understanding of the world is the goal of each "For Thought and Discussion" exercise. Discussion tips and subject helps for the teacher are available in the teacher notes. But, it is most helpful for the teacher to be intimately familiar with the subject matter. Reading along with the student is recommended.

Lastly, the goal of learning 'wisdom' is encouraged through application and communication. This is done in the "Writing and Thinking" exercises at the end of each Test. In the "Writing and Thinking" exercises the student is asked to communicate in a clear and precise manner their application of select "For Thought and Discussion" exercises. This exercise will not be difficult IF the teacher has been diligent enough to guide the student through the "For Thought and Discussion" exercises.

With this method of learning, both teacher and student must be persistent. The exercises take work. But in the end, the student will reap a bounty of knowledge, understanding and wisdom to the glory of God.

Suggested Additional Reading for American Literature LIFEPAC 1

Iain H. Murray, *Jonathan Edwards: A New Biography*
(Edinburgh: The Banner of Truth Trust, 1987).

James I. Packer, *A Quest for Godliness: The Puritan Vision of the Christian Life*
(Grand Rapids, MI: Zondervan Publishing House, 1991).

The Autobiography of Benjamin Franklin, ed. J. A. Leo LeMay and Paul M. Zall
(New York: W.W. Norton & Company, 1979).

The Poems of Edward Taylor, ed. Donald Stanford
(Chapel Hill, NC: University of North Carolina Press, 1989).

The Works of Anne Bradstreet, ed. Jeannine Hensley
(Cambridge, MA: The Belknap Press of Harvard University Press, 1967).

The Works of Jonathan Edwards, vols. 2, ed. Edward Hickman
(Edinburgh: The Banner of Truth Trust, 1974.)

Suggested Additional Reading for LIFEPAC 2

Alexis de Tocqueville, *Democracy in America*, vols. 2, trans. Henry Reeve
(New York: Vintage Books, 1954).

F.O. Matthiessen, *American Renaissance; art and expression in the age of Emerson and Whitman*
(London: Oxford University Press, 1941).

Nathaniel Hawthorne, *The Scarlet Letter*
(New York : Vintage Books, 1990).

Herman Melville, *Moby Dick*
(Oxford: Oxford University Press, 1998).

Emily Dickinson, *The Complete Poems*
(Boston: Little, Brown, 1960).

Suggested Additional Reading for LIFEPAC 3

Fredrick Douglas, *Narrative of the Life of Fredrick Douglas: An American Slave*
(Boston: Harvard, 1967).

Harriet Beecher Stowe, *Uncle Tom's Cabin*
(New York: Garland, 1994).

Burke Davis, *Gray Fox: Robert E. Lee and the Civil War*
(Burford Books, 1998).

The Life and Writings of Abraham Lincoln, ed. Philip Van Stern
(New York: Random House, 1999).

Mark Twain, *The Adventures of Huckleberry Finn*
(New York: Penguin Group, 1985).

Henry James, *The Portrait of a Lady*
(New York: Bantam Doubleday Dell Publishing Group, Incorporated, 1983).

Stephen Crane, *The Red Badge of Courage*
(New York: Bantam Doubleday Dell Publishing Group, Inc., 1981).

Materials Needed for LIFEPAC 4
    Required:
        Our Town by Thornton Wilder

Suggested Additional Readings for LIFEPAC 4
    Ernest Hemingway, *The Old Man and the Sea*
    (New York: Simon & Schuster Inc., 1995).

    F. Scott Fitzgerald, *The Great Gatsby*
    (New York: Simon & Schuster, 1996).

    Robert Frost, *Poems*
    (New York: Penguin Group, 1989).

    Langston Hughes, *The Collected Poems of Langston Hughes*
    (New York: Vintage Books, 1995).

    J. Gresham Machen, *Christianity and Liberalism*
    (Grand Rapids, MI: William B. Eerdmans, 1990).

Suggested Additional Reading for LIFEPAC 5

    Gene Edward Veith, *Postmodern Times: A Christian's Guide to Contemporary Thought and Culture*
    (Wheaton, IL: Crossway Books, 1994).

    Flannery O'Connor, *The Complete Stories*
    (New York: Farrar, Straus and Giroux, 1984).

    Eudora Welty, *A Curtain of Green and Other Stories*
    (Harcourt Brace & Company, 1979).

Selected Bibliography

    Listed below are writings that have been used and consulted in the creation of this work. It is not a complete listing of the sources consulted.

    Gene Edward Veith, *Reading Between the Lines: A Christian's Guide to Literature*
    (Wheaton, IL: Crossway Books, 1990).

    Invitation to the Classics, ed. Louise Cowan and Os Guinness
    (Grand Rapids, MI: Baker Books, 1998).

    Mark Noll, *A History of Christianity in the United States and Canada*
    (Grand Rapids, MI: William B. Eerdmans Publishing Company, 1992).

    Richard Ruland and Malcolm Bradbury, *From Puritanism to Postmodernism*
    (New York: Viking Penguin, 1991).

    The Norton Anthology of American Literature, vol. 1 & 2, ed.
    Ronald Gottesman and Francis Murphy
    (New York: W.W. Norton & Company, 1979).

    William Harmon and C. Hugh Holman, Handbook to Literature
    (Upper Saddle River, NJ: Prentice Hall, 1996).

American Literature-Related Web Sites
    American Literature A to Z <https://www.americanliterature.com/home>
    Short story project <https://www.shortstoryproject.com>
    Early American Literature 1600-1900 <http://falcon.jmu.edu/~ramseyil/amlit.htm>
    Project Gutenberg Index <http://www.mirrors.org.sg/pg/>

T E S T S

Reproducible Tests
for use with the American Literature
Teacher's Guide

AMERICAN LITERATURE LIFEPAC ONE ALTERNATE TEST

Name _____

Date _____

Score _____

80/100

Fill in each of the blanks using items from the following word list (each answer, 1 point).

actions	analyze	sovereignty
Bible	change	Pocahontas
God	providential	history
King Philip's	God	

1. Christians must think about and _____ what an author is trying to say about _____ , humanity and the world, always comparing what we read with the timeless truths of Scripture.

2. The Puritans viewed the _____ as their sole guide to faith and life.

3. The core of Puritan beliefs was based upon the doctrine of God's _____ .

4. The story of _____ did not appear in Smith's earlier records of life in Virginia.

5. Bradford wrote *Of Plymouth Plantation* to preserve the _____ of the Pilgrims' plight and God's _____ care.

6. Mary Rowlandson's Narrative is the deeply personal account of her sufferings during _____ war.

7. Anne Bradstreet concludes in her poem "In Memory of My Dear Grandchild" that _____ is in control of her grandchild's fate.

8. Edward Taylor, in the poem "Huswifery," asks the Lord to _____ him so that his words and _____ glorify God.

Answer *true* or *false* for each of the following statements (each answer, 2 points).

9. _____ The Indians helped Mrs. Rowlandson heal her wounded child.

10. _____ An Indian gave Mrs. Rowlandson a Bible while she was in captivity.

11. _____ After her captivity, Mrs. Rowlandson is able to see that when God calls a person to anything He will fully be able to carry them through and make them see that they have benefited from the experience.

12. _____ In "Contemplations," Bradstreet realizes her ignorance in not seeing the glory of God all around her.

13. _____ The "we" in "To My Dear and Loving Husband" refers to Bradstreet and her husband.

14. _____ The pilgrim that Bradstreet describes in "A Weary Pilgrim" is herself.

15. _____ In his diary, Sewall only discusses his spiritual growth.

Underline the correct answer in each of the following statements (each answer, 2 points).

16. Anne Bradstreet's (brother-in-law, brother, husband) had her books published without her knowledge.

17. Edward Taylor was forced to sail to America because he would not sign an oath of loyalty to the (Church of England, Puritans, Pope).

18. For over fifty years, Taylor served as (journalist, minister, carpenter) physician, and civil servant to a community 100 miles west of Boston.

19. Samuel Sewall's Diary is a detailed record of life in (Florida, New England, England).

20. Sewall's life reflects the trend (away from, toward) materialism and (away from, toward) exclusively religious concerns.

Answer *true* or *false* for each of the following statements (each answer, 1 point).

21. _____ William Bradford set out to write *Of Plymouth Plantation* in an ornate style, with singular regard unto complex lies about all things.

22. _____ During the first winter, only two Puritans died.

23. _____ As a "city upon a hill," Winthrop reminded the Puritans that the eyes of the world would be watching to see if they would be faithful to God.

24. _____ If the Puritans were not faithful to God, Winthrop proclaimed that they would not succeed in America.

25. _____ Sir Isaac Newton and John Locke opened the world's eyes to a universe governed by natural laws.

26. _____ The New Science was oriented toward superstitious beliefs.

27. _____ According to Deists, man is the master of his own destiny.

28. _____ Revival struck Edwards' congregation while he was preaching the Puritan doctrines of salvation.

29. _____ Thomas Paine's *Common Sense* helped start the French Revolution.

30. _____ From childhood up, Edwards never doubted the doctrine of God's sovereignty in salvation.

31. _____ Edwards viewed his sin as "an abyss infinitely deeper than hell."

32. _____ Prior to the Great Awakening, Franklin describes Americans as being "thoughtless or indifferent about religion."

33. _____ The Declaration of Independence stated that it was not necessary for the American people to "dissolve the political bands" with the British.

34. _____ The three "unalienable rights" are Life, Liberty and the pursuit of Wealth.

Underline the correct answer in each of the following statements (each answer, 2 points).

35. The Puritans were (a large, a small, the only) group that migrated to America during the 17th century.

36. The literary life of the Puritans grew out of a need for (uselessness, practicality, idleness).

37. To the Puritan, history was a revelation of (Man's, God's, Satan's) plan for human existence.

38. Puritan literature is filled with comparisons between themselves and the (English, Israelites, Russians).

39. The purpose of the Puritan literary style was to tell (the truth, stories, lies) as simply and plainly as possible.

40. Mrs. Rowlandson's story created a new form of writing called the (Faithful Wife narrative, Indian-captivity narrative, Pirate narrative).

41. It was aboard the (*Mayflower, Cambridge, Arbella*) that John Winthrop composed the sermon "A Model of Christian Charity."

42. The Massachusetts Bay Colony sought to establish a (tyrannical, democratic, theocratic) form of government.

Fill in each of the blanks using items from the following word list (each answer, 2 points).

advancement	stands	influential
French	God	center
grace	hands	life

43. "There is nothing that keeps wicked men at any one moment out of hell, but the mere pleasure of _____."

44. "God has made no promises either of eternal _____, or of any deliverance from eternal death, but what are contained in the covenant of _____, the promises that are given in Christ.

45. "All you that were never born again, and made new creatures, and raised from being dead in sin, to a state of new, and before altogether unexperienced light and life, are in the _____ of an angry God."

46. Franklin's *Autobiography* is a story of materialistic and social _____.

47. For Franklin, God was not at the _____ of life, man was.

48. Thomas Paine was the most _____ political writer of the Revolution.

49. "The summer soldier and the sunshine patriot will, in this crisis, shrink from the service of their country; but he that _____ it now, deserves the love and thanks of man and woman."

50. Crèvecoeur was a _____ immigrant.

Underline the correct answer in each of the following statements (each answer, 3 points).

51. Jonathan Edwards has been described as the most astute scholar that (Spain, Canada, America) has produced.

52. (Man's, God's, Satan's) sovereignty in salvation and in the world was an integral aspect to Edwards' beliefs.

53. Jefferson thought that (human reason, the Scriptures, superstition) was the supreme authority in matters of belief and conduct.

54. In describing American society, Crèvecoeur writes "it is not composed, as in Europe, of great lords who possess (nothing, everything, something) and of a herd of people who have (everything, nothing)."

AMERICAN LITERATURE LIFEPAC TWO ALTERNATE TEST

Name _____

Date _____

Score _____

80 / 100

Answer *true* or *false* for each of the following statements (each answer, 1 point).

1. _____ Europe was the standard by which American society and culture were judged.

2. _____ America writers complained that the vast open landscape put limitations on what they could write about.

3. _____ Romanticism focused on the individual's imagination and feelings.

4. _____ Romanticism replaced God's Word with reason.

5. _____ According to the Romantic, nature was innocent and man was essentially good.

6. _____ In Cooper's novel, *The Prairie*, Middleton and Paul find Natty Bumpoo approaching death.

7. _____ In Bryant's poem, *Thanaposis*, the speaker says that if the thought of death makes you "grow sick at heart" you should listen to Nature.

8. _____ In *Thanaposis*, Bryant encourages the reader to be "sustained and soothed" because death will bring nothing more than "pleasant dreams."

Fill in each of the blanks using items from the following word list (each answer, 2 points).

William Wordsworth	German	writer
henpecked	petticoat	Catskill
Romantic	twenty	

9. Rip Van Winkle's village was founded by Dutch colonists in the _____ mountains.

10. Rip was a kind neighbor, and an obedient _____ husband.

11. Rip slept for _____ years.

12. Rip was happy to be freed from the tyranny of Dame Van Winkle, which he called the _____ government.

13. Washington Irving was the first American to achieve international fame as a

_____ .

14. By placing _____ folktales in an American setting, Irving gave America a legendary past.

15. Bryant's poems helped to establish the _____ movement in America.

16. Bryant has been likened to the British poet _____ .

Answer *true* or *false* for each of the following statements (each answer, 2 points).

17. _____ American literature was truly born between 1770–1800.

18. _____ America continued to experience rapid growth and expansion between 1840–1855.

19. _____ Transcendentalism believed that everything was connected spiritually by a universal being.

20. _____ Transcendentalists taught that man was essentially bad.

21. _____ The Bible was the Scriptures of the transcendentalists.

22. _____ Melville, Hawthorne, Poe and Dickinson's views on man and the world did not agree with transcendental beliefs.

23. _____ Longfellow, Whittier, and Holmes were Fireside poets.

24. _____ The American Naissance ended with the advent of World War I.

Underline the correct answer in each of the following statements (each answer, 1 point).

25. James Fenimore Cooper was America's first (poet, novelist, politician).

26. In The Leatherstocking Tales, Cooper creates America's first fictional (mother, outcast, hero).

27. Longfellow's work fostered a national interest in (the novel, poetry, the short story).

28. Longfellow Americanized European (legends, rhythm, myths).

29. Whittier was a devout (Baptist, Unitarian, Quaker) and a passionate (Southerner, abolitionist, non-conformist).

30. *Snowbound* is a faithful poetic narrative of American (farm, city, frontier) life.

31. In Whittier's poem, *Snowbound*, the snow covered landscape inspires a feeling of (amazement, fear, indifference).

32. Oliver Wendell Holmes was a professor of (English, business, medicine) at Dartmouth College and Harvard University.

33. After retirement from the medical profession, Holmes became a popular (stand-up comedian, politician, dinner speaker) and occasional poet.

34. Ralph Waldo Emerson's beliefs took the (Pessimistic, Biblical, Romantic) Movement one step further.

35. Emerson disbelieved in the (goodness, ability, sinfulness) of man and the deity of (himself, Jesus, man).

36. Emerson was ordained as a (Unitarian, Baptist, Pentecostal) preacher.

37. (Thoreau and Whitman, Melville and Hawthorne, Dickinson and Poe) took Emerson's philosophy to its logical end.

Fill in each of the blanks using items from the following word list (each answer, 1 point).

free verse	institutions	wave
resist	rhyme	Walden Pond
transcendental	sublime	shift

38. Longfellow states, in his poem, A Psalm of Life, that the lives of great men teach us that "we can make our lives _____."

39. According to the last stanza of Holmes' poem "Old Ironsides," the best end for the ship would be to "sink beneath the _____."

40. Thoreau rejected established society and its _____.

41. For two years, Thoreau lived alone in a cabin at _____, testing the validity of his _____ beliefs.

42. Thoreau thought that a person should _____ all laws that his conscience did not agree with.

43. Whitman was the first American to write poetry in _____.

44. Free verse lines do not _____.

45. Whitman's work caused a significant moral _____ in American literature.

Answer *true* **or** *false* **for each of the following statements** (each answer, 2 points).

46. _____ Emerson believed he was "part or parcel of God."

47. _____ Thoreau cries for "simplicity, simplicity, simplicity" because he believes our lives are wasted by worrying about details.

48. _____ Thoreau leaves the woods because his cabin burns down.

49. _____ In *Song of Myself*, Whitman celebrates the God of the Bible.

50. _____ A child asks, "What is grass?" in Whitman's poem.

Underline the correct answer in each of the following statements (each answer, 1 point).

51. Nathaniel Hawthorne was haunted by the (happiness, guilt, contentment) of his ancestors.

52. He is both sympathetic and critical of (transcendental, Puritan, Hindu) beliefs.

53. Herman Melville's life and work was marked with despair and (enthusiasm, frustration, happiness).

54. He sought out the friendship of (Poe, Hawthorne, Dickinson).

55. Melville's work was not appreciated until the (1890s, 1920s, 1980s).

Fill in each of the blanks using items from the following word list (each answer, 1 point).

world	happiness	untraditional
Horror	Lenore	single
melancholy	nevermore	Aidenn
Philadelphia	seven	

56. In "The Raven," the speaker feels sorrow for a "radiant maiden" named _____.

57. The only word that the raven says is _____.

58. The turning point in the poem occurs when the speaker asks the raven if Lenore will be in heaven, which he calls _____.

59. His literary career was spread between Baltimore, Richmond, New York, and _____.

60. Poe tried to convey a _____ mood or emotion in each work.

61. _____ dominates Poe's fiction and _____ pervades his poetry.

62.   Emily Dickinson wrote in an _____ form.

63.   Only _____ of Dickinson's poems were published during her lifetime.

64.   Dickinson looked for _____ in the things of this _____ but only found lasting bitterness.

Answer *true* **or** *false* **for each of the following statements** (each answer, 1 point).

65.   _____ In "The Whiteness of the Whale," Ishmael claims that the fear, awe and reverence he feels for the appearance of white is an instinctive reaction, much like that of the frightened colt with a buffalo robe on his back.

66.   _____ According to the last two paragraphs and the introduction of the "Whiteness of the Whale," the White Whale symbolizes the holiness of God.

67.   _____ The whale is hunted because its color and its symbolism make it one of the things "most appalling to mankind."

68.   _____ In Hawthorne' short story, *The Minister's Black Veil,* the members of Mr. Hooper's congregation are amazed and astonished when they first see the black veil on his face.

69.   _____ Mr. Hooper tells Elizabeth that the veil is a type and a symbol and that he cannot remove it while on earth.

70.   _____ The black veil symbolizes sin.

71.   _____ The story is a parable about man's sinfulness and his unwillingness to acknowledge it.

72.   _____ In Dickinson's poem, "This is my letter to the World," the speaker is talking only to her family.

73.   _____ In "The Bustle in the House," the activity in a house the "morning after death" is described as the merriest thing on earth.

74.   _____ In "Hope," fear "perches in the soul."

AMERICAN LITERATURE LIFEPAC THREE ALTERNATE TEST

Name _____

Date _____

Score _____

82 / 102

Fill in each of the blanks using items from the following word list (each answer, 4 points).

Fredrick Douglass'   North   meaningless
southerners   William Dean Howells   free
hymns   musical   Stephen Crane
dies

1. _____ saw the value in writing about ordinary people and encouraged other writers to do so.

2. Black spirituals are a combination of African _____ patterns and Protestant _____ .

3. The Emancipation Proclamation declared every slave forever _____ .

4. _____ ability to read and write encouraged his desire for freedom.

5. _____ was one of the first naturalistic writers.

6. Crane believed that life was accidental and _____ .

7. When Mrs. Mallard sees that her husband is alive, she _____ .

8. Robert E. Lee encouraged fellow _____ to accept defeat graciously.

9. Many of the black spirituals contained secret directions to the _____ .

Underline the correct answer in each of the following statements (each answer, 2 points).

10. *Uncle Tom's Cabin* has been one of the most read (poems, speeches, novels) of American literature.

11. In his letter to his son, Robert E. Lee described secession as nothing but (revolution, anarchy, peace).

12. In the "Gettysburg Address," Lincoln resolved not to let the (religion, government) of the people, by the people and for the people perish from the earth.

13. Mark Twain's use of (formal, traditional, colloquial) language in his books displayed elements of Realism and Regionalism.

14. (Stephen Crane, Henry James, Ernest Hemingway) emphasized the importance and use of a character's point-of-view.

15. Kate Chopin stories question the traditional roles of (men, women, children) in society and marriage.

16. Most of Chopin's stories are set in (Louisiana, New Jersey, San Francisco).

17. Paul Laurence Dunbar was the first (white, black, Irish) American to achieve an international reputation as a poet.

18. Dunbar excelled in (modern, ancient, traditional) forms of poetry and also wrote in black American dialect.

19. London became one of the highest paid (gold miners, writers, salesmen) of his time.

20. London's stories express a strong (evolutionary, Christian, Catholic) and socialistic view of the world.

Answer *true* **or** *false* **for each of the following statements** (each answer, 2 points).

21. _____ The North and the South were founded on two different economic and social systems.

22. _____ Both the North and the South disbelieved that God was on their side.

23. _____ Prior to the Civil War, America was an industrialized nation.

24. _____ The South relied heavily on slave labor.

25. _____ The revivalists of the Second Awakening preached very similar to those of the Great Awakening.

26. _____ The cause for abolition, women's suffrage, and temperance were all intimately connected to the revivals of the 19th century.

27. _____ America experienced great changes during the period between the Civil War and World War I.

28. _____ Inherent within the theory of evolution is the notion that man is developing physically and morally into a perfect being.

29. _____ Realism presented a romantic view of the world.

30. _____ Naturalism reflected the influence of Dwight L. Moody's sermons on society and culture.

31. _____ Regionalism attempted to capture the details of life in a specific region of the country.

32. _____ Douglass' "victory" over Mr. Covey signified a turning point in his life as a slave and renewed his determination to become free.

33. _____ After Huck makes his decision to "take up wickedness again," he decides to leave Jim in bondage.

34. _____ Editha personifies society and its traditionally held belief that fighting in a war brings a man dishonor.

35. _____ Winterbourne thinks of Daisy as a pretty, Italian flirt.

36. _____ In *The Red Badge of Courage*, the youth burned to enlist because he had heard there was much glory in the marches, sieges, and conflicts.

37. _____ Before the battle, as the youth lays in his bunk, he begins to worry that he will run out of food.

38. _____ The souls of those that wear the mask are sorrowful and tormented.

39. _____ Koskoosh is left behind in the snow because he is old and can longer walk.

40. _____ Before Koskoosh is killed he remembers that his son is coming back for him.

AMERICAN LITERATURE LIFEPAC FOUR ALTERNATE TEST

Name _____

Date _____

Score _____

85 / 106

Fill in each of the blanks using items from the following word list (each answer, 2 points).

emptiness	American	unconventional
rhythm	religion	scenery
clear	cultural	reality
satire	adjectives	

1. Ernest Hemingway's writing style is _____ and precise.

2. Hemingway avoided _____ and focused on the weight of his nouns.

3. F. Scott Fitzgerald's characters are troubled by an _____ they cannot fulfill.

4. Unable to find an answer to the world's problems in politics, W. H. Auden turned to

    _____ .

5. *"The Unknown Citizen"* is a _____ of modern problems.

6. The poetry of Langston Hughes captures the _____ of jazz and blues.

7. Hughes inspired other black writers to be proud of their _____ roots.

8. His work helped to provide a lasting place for black writers in _____ literature.

9. No curtains and little _____ are not used in Wilder's plays, making them _____ .

10. Wilder never wanted his audience to forget that the play they were watching was not

    _____ .

Answer *true* **or** *false* **for each of the following statements** (each answer, 2 points).

11. _____ At the heart of the Fundamentalist/Modernist controversy was the Bible.

12. _____ World War I proved that society and its traditional beliefs and manners had failed.

13. _____ After World War I, art began to reflect the pessimism and discontinuity of the modern age.

14. _____ Modernism assumed that the world had moved into a post-Christian era.

15. _____ In Ernest Hemingway's short story, "In Another Country," the hospital patients are hooked up to machines in order to heal their wounds.

16. _____ In F. Scott Fitzgerald's short story, "Winter Dreams," Dexter Green's winter-dreams were concerned with the attainment of "glittering things."

17. _____ Faces are compared to petals on a tree branch in the poem, "In a Station of the Metro."

18. _____ In his poem "Chicago," Carl Sandburg uses long lines of free verse.

19. _____ In the poem, "Anecdote of the Jar," the jar shapes reality.

20. _____ In Frost's poem, "Mending Wall," the neighbor's only response to the speaker is, "Good fences make good neighbors."

21. _____ In "The Unknown Citizen," W. H. Auden is criticizing modern society because it is too personal.

22. _____ In "The Trumpet Player," the music is described as "honey/ Mixed with liquid fire."

23. _____ The rhythm is described as "agony/ Distilled from new desire."

24. _____ In the play, "Our Town," the stage directions call for an elaborate curtain.

25. _____ The Stage Manager tells the audience that in the future Joe Crowell, Jr. dies in France during the war.

26. _____ Mr. Webb describes Grover's Corners as a very ordinary town.

27. _____ The Stage Manager wants to get a copy of the play placed in the cornerstone of the new bank so that people a thousand years from now will know a few simple facts about Grover's Corners.

28. _____ The Christian gospel is an account of how man saves himself.

29. _____ Liberalism and Christianity have identical concepts of God and man.

30. _____ Christianity begins with the consciousness of sin.

31. _____ Salvation, according to the Bible, depends upon an event that happened long ago.

32 _____ Liberalism is founded upon the shifting emotions of sinful men, otherwise known as "experience."

33. _____ At the center of Liberalism is the doctrine of "justification by faith."

34. _____ Liberalism says that our obedience to God's law is the ground of hope.

Underline the correct answer in each of the following statements (each answer, 2 points).

35. The modernist style (expands, exaggerates, compresses) emotion and narration.

36. The modernist movement saw truth as a matter of (biblical standard, historical record, interpretation).

37. Black writers of the Harlem Renaissance carried the rhythms of (Baroque, classical, jazz and blues) music over into various forms of literature.

38. Ezra Pound's experimental techniques and forms had no regard for (traditional, modern, progressive) ideas and approaches.

39. Pound was a central figure in the (Modernist, Traditionalist, Fundamentalist) movement.

40. Pound's most influential form of poetry was called (traditionalism, imagism, communism).

41. Imagism focused on concrete (impressions, images, types) rather than abstractions.

42. Carl Sandburg wrote about the struggles and triumphs of the (middle, working, upper) class.

43. Sandburg's use of (free, traditional, experimental) verse form made his poems easy to grasp.

44. E. E. Cummings used (traditional, experimental, orthodox) forms to view the familiar in a new way.

45. Wallace Stevens believed that (worship, poetry, singing) was the highest human activity.

46. According to Stevens, the imagination of (God, man) is that which shapes reality.

47. As a traditional poet, Frost believed poetry should begin in (pain, agony, delight) and end with (wisdom, confusion, ignorance).

48. Frost's poems are replete with images of (city life, farm life, modern decay).

49. As an advocate of the (inaccuracy, inerrancy, myth) of Scripture, J. Gresham Machen was (liberalism's, fundamentalism's, modernism's) "most prominent champion" in the 1930's.

50. *Christianity and Liberalism,* Machen's most well-known book, argued that (fundamentalists, modernists) were not preaching the gospel but had created a new religion.

AMERICAN LITERATURE LIFEPAC FIVE ALTERNATE TEST

Name _____

Date _____

Score _____

75 / 94

In this test, the term 'Negro' will be used because it is a direct quote. In no way is this term meant to be disrespectful.

Fill in each of the blanks using items from the following word list (each answer, 2 points).

traditional	breathing	community
Egypt	grotesque	lose
middle-class	Mohand as K. Gandhi	Moses
peace	poetry	Brooks'
valued	postmodern	pride
social	societal	stream-of-consciousness
truth		

1. In postmodern society, a universal standard of _____ no longer exists.

2. Societies that stop believing in a universal standard of truth tend to _____ their ability to create great pieces of art.

3. Fiction writers from the south have produced works that have been called _____ .

4. Novels and short stories of the _____ era show elements of traditional works.

5. The _____ technique continues to be used in postmodern writing.

6. Roethke _____ traditional forms of poetry.

7. The works of black writers reflect a need for _____ change.

8. Roethke's poems are a reflection of his spiritual quest for _____ and understanding.

9. According to line 11 of Roethke's poem the "Root Cellar," even dirt—a seemingly lifeless thing—kept _____ .

10. John Updike focuses upon the everyday life of the _____ .

11. Updike's stories diagnose _____ and personal ills while offering a religious and moral cure.

12. Dr. Martin Luther King, Jr. adopted the nonviolent protest philosophy of _____ .

13. Dr. Martin Luther King, Jr. often compared himself to _____ and his people's difficulties to ancient Israel's enslavement to _____ .

14.   Chicago and its black society are the subject matter of much of _____ poetry.

15.   Brooks' most recent work reflects a push towards black _____ and _____ .

16.   Much of Brooks' poetry is written in _____ form.

17.   The most popular _____ to emerge during the postmodern era has been written in traditional form.

Answer *true* or *false* for each of the following statements (each answer, 2 points).

18.   _____   In the short story, "The Displaced Person," Mrs. Shortley believed that Mr. Guizac was from the devil.

19.   _____   Mrs. McIntyre believed that "Christ was just another D.P."

20.   _____   The Guizacs are from a foreign country.

21.   _____   The priest declares that he is not theological but practical.

22.   _____   In Eudora Welty's short story, "A Worn Path," Phoenix Jackson makes the long journey to get medicine for her grandson.

23.   _____   In Updike's short story, "Separating," Dickie was most nearly Richard's conscience.

24.   _____   Martin Luther King. Jr. had a dream that one day the nation would live out the true meaning of its creed: "We hold these truths to be self-evident, that all men are created equal."

25.   _____   Martin Luther King quotes two songs in his "I Have a Dream" speech: a Negro spiritual and "America."

26.   _____   In Ellison's book, *Invisible Man,* the speaker says that he is an invisible man because people refuse to see him.

27.   _____   The old woman and the invisible man become confused over what is freedom.

28.   _____   The invisible man refuses to take responsibility for the near murder.

29.   _____   According to line 5 of Brook's poem, "Lovers of the Poor," the ladies have proud faces.

30.   _____   The ladies only want to give to anyone who needs it.

31.   _____   According to lines 90–92, the ladies refuse to give their "loathe-love" because there is no hope of change.

Underline the correct answer in each of the following statements (each answer, 2 points).

32.   Eudora Welty's stories capture the details of life in the deep (South, East, North).

33.   The Modern Age searched for truth apart from (Christianity, Communism, Marxism).

34.   The French Revolution exalted (human reason, divine revelation, the Bible).

35.   (Existentialism, Christianity, Marxism) is the belief that people have unlimited freedom of choice.

36.   (God, Man, Government) alone is the author of truth.

37.   In the technological age, the (television, Bible, reason) became the great authenticator of truth.

38.   Existentialism is directly opposed to (Christian, Marxist, democratic) thought.

39.   The (medieval, modern, postmodern) age began with the French Revolution.

40.   Robert Lowell's poetry is marked by public and personal (consistency, change, evenness).

41.   Flannery O'Connor's stories paint a realistic picture of man's (purity, sinfulness, happiness).

42.   Frustrated, the speaker in Lowell's poem "Epilogue," says that his work is like a (snapshot, portrait, watch).

43.   According to line 20 of Lowell's poem "Epilogue," people are "poor passing (creatures, facts, beings)."

44.   Ellison has proclaimed himself to be a (writer, speaker, lecturer) rather than a spokesman.

45.   The *Invisible Man* is about all (Asians, Africans, Americans) and their search for self and being.

**A
N
S
W
E
R

K
E
Y
S**

SECTION ONE

1.1	thoughts, beliefs
1.2	analyze, God
1.3	good
1.4	Massachusetts
1.5	a small
1.6	Separatists
1.7	Non-separatists
1.8	Non-separatists
1.9	Christian
1.10	Bible
1.11	Sovereignty
1.12	joys, God
1.13	humble
1.14	Pilgrims, individual, colony
1.15	Constitution
1.16	state, governed
1.17	work
1.18	industry
1.19	novel, time
1.20	practicality
1.21	God's
1.22	Israelites
1.23	typology
1.24	Scripture
1.25	the truth
1.26	creative
1.27	Anne Bradstreet's
1.28	Indian-captivity narrative
1.29	American
1.30	explorer
1.31	John Smith
1.32	New England
1.33	Pocahontas
1.34	gold and copper
1.35	not everyone
1.36	savages
1.37	water, castles
1.38	savages
1.39	weak, industry
1.40	Indians (or Native Americans), Chickahominy
1.41	Pocahontas, head
1.42	Robinson, Emery
1.43	13

1.44	separatists
1.45	65
1.46	30
1.47	history, providential
1.48	F
1.49	T
1.50	F
1.51	T
1.52	F
1.53	T
1.54	F
1.55	T
1.56	Scriptures
1.57	could be
1.58	lawyer
1.59	*Arbella*
1.60	theocratic
1.61	F
1.62	T
1.63	T
1.64	T

SECTION TWO

2.1	King Philip's
2.2	mother
2.3	popular
2.4	sovereignty

2.5	T
2.6	F
2.7	F
2.8	T
2.9	F
2.10	T
2.11	F
2.12	T
2.13	T

2.14	received
2.15	eight
2.16	brother-in-law
2.17	similar to
2.18	unfeigned

2.19	F
2.20	T
2.21	T
2.22	T
2.23	T
2.24	F

2.25	flower
2.26	guides
2.27	God

2.28	T
2.29	F
2.30	T
2.31	F

2.32	Church of England
2.33	minister
2.34	strong

2.35	Lord
2.36	actions
2.37	holy

2.38	New England
2.39	toward, away from
2.40	business

2.41	F
2.42	T
2.43	T

SECTION THREE

3.1	F
3.2	T
3.3	T
3.4	F
3.5	T
3.6	F
3.7	T
3.8	T
3.9	F
3.10	T
3.11	T
3.12	T
3.13	F
3.14	F
3.15	T
3.16	F
3.17	T
3.18	T
3.19	T
3.20	T

3.21	America
3.22	ministers
3.23	hours
3.24	Awakening
3.25	God's
3.26	faith
3.27	small pox

3.28	T
3.29	T
3.30	F
3.31	F
3.32	T
3.33	F
3.34	T
3.35	T
3.36	F

3.37	God
3.38	ruin, restraint
3.39	prudence, lives
3.40	life, death, grace, Christ
3.41	hell's, pleasure
3.42	new, hands
3.43	mercy, sinners
3.44	awake, wrath

3.45	self-made
3.46	3
3.47	student
3.48	self-improvement
3.49	advancement
3.50	center

3.51	difficult
3.52	temperance, industry, humility
3.53	different writers
3.54	shows the means of obtaining virtue

3.55	T
3.56	T
3.57	F
3.58	T
3.59	T
3.60	F

3.61	1774
3.62	persuasive
3.63	England
3.64	120,000
3.65	France
3.66	ridicule
3.67	deist
3.68	church

3.69	shrink, stands, thanks
3.70	Britain, help
3.71	governs, happy, dominion
3.72	all, every, force
3.73	perseverance

3.74	architect
3.75	human reason
3.76	*Summary View*
3.77	protect, tyrannical
3.78	third

3.79	F
3.80	F
3.81	F
3.82	T
3.83	F
3.84	T

3.85	Canada
3.86	British
3.87	New York
3.88	French
3.89	citizen

3.90	everything, nothing
3.91	European
3.92	wildness

SECTION ONE

1.1	T
1.2	F
1.3	F
1.4	F
1.5	F
1.6	F
1.7	T
1.8	F
1.9	T
1.10	F
1.11	T
1.12	F

1.13	writer
1.14	New York
1.15	German
1.16	entertain
1.17	human

1.18	Catskill
1.19	henpecked
1.20	idleness
1.21	woods
1.22	sleep
1.23	twenty
1.24	foot
1.25	George Washington
1.26	petticoat

1.27	novelist
1.28	wife
1.29	hero
1.30	social

1.31	F
1.32	T
1.33	T
1.34	F
1.35	T
1.36	F

1.37	Romantic
1.38	women's rights, political
1.39	graveyard poets
1.40	William Wordsworth

1.41	T
1.42	F
1.43	T
1.44	F
1.45	T

SECTION TWO

2.1	T
2.2	F
2.3	F
2.4	T
2.5	F
2.6	T
2.7	T
2.8	F
2.9	F
2.10	T
2.11	F
2.12	T
2.13	F
2.14	T
2.15	F
2.16	T
2.17	F

2.18	common man
2.19	teaching
2.20	the poem
2.21	modern
2.22	rhythms
2.23	optimistic
2.24	real, earnest
2.25	future, Act
2.26	sublime
2.27	heart

2.28	poor, little
2.29	Quaker, abolitionist
2.30	physical
2.31	Christian love
2.32	farm
2.33	east
2.34	do their nightly chores
2.35	amazement
2.36	solitude
2.37	secure

2.38	medicine
2.39	literary magazine
2.40	Jonathan Edwards
2.41	novels

2.42	dinner speaker
2.43	heroes', foe
2.44	more
2.45	flood
2.46	wave

2.47	Romantic
2.48	enthusiastic
2.49	sinfulness, Jesus
2.50	Unitarian
2.51	biblical
2.52	traditional
2.53	Thoreau and Whitman

2.54	T
2.55	F
2.56	F
2.57	F

2.58	self-reliance
2.59	institutions
2.60	Walden Pond, transcendental
2.61	resist
2.62	social activists

2.63	F
2.64	F
2.65	F
2.66	T
2.67	F

2.68	moral
2.69	himself
2.70	lazy
2.71	unrestrained
2.72	nurse
2.73	free verse
2.74	rhyme
2.75	shift

2.76	F
2.77	T
2.78	T
2.79	T
2.80	T

SECTION THREE

3.1   two
3.2   son
3.3   gambling
3.4   Philadelphia
3.5   success
3.6   single
3.7   Horror, melancholy

3.8   visitor
3.9   Lenore
3.10   window, Pallas
3.11   nevermore
3.12   Aidenn
3.13   heart, door
3.14   demon

3.15   guilt
3.16   Puritan
3.17   Salem
3.18   consul
3.19   guilt

3.20   T
3.21   F
3.22   F
3.23   T
3.24   F
3.25   T
3.26   F
3.27   T
3.28   T
3.29   T

3.30   frustration
3.31   life
3.32   success
3.33   decline
3.34   Hawthorne
3.35   New York
3.36   1920s

3.37   T
3.38   T
3.39   F
3.40   T
3.41   T
3.42   F
3.43   T
3.44   T

3.45   untraditional
3.46   seven
3.47   Amherst
3.48   isolated
3.49   happiness, world

3.50   F
3.51   T
3.52   F
3.53   F
3.54   F
3.55   T
3.56   F
3.57   F
3.58   F
3.59   T

SECTION ONE

1.1	T
1.2	T
1.3	F
1.4	F
1.5	F
1.6	T
1.7	F
1.8	F
1.9	T
1.10	T
1.11	T
1.12	T
1.13	F
1.14	F
1.15	T
1.16	T
1.17	F
1.18	T
1.19	T
1.20	F
1.21	F
1.22	F
1.23	F

1.24	read, write
1.25	abolitionist
1.26	Great Britain
1.27	Union
1.28	discriminated

1.29	T
1.30	F
1.31	T
1.32	T
1.33	T
1.34	F
1.35	T
1.36	T
1.37	F
1.38	F
1.39	T
1.40	F

1.41	Abraham Lincoln
1.42	most
1.43	Abolitionist
1.44	*Uncle Tom's Cabin*
1.45	500,000
1.46	romantic

1.47	F
1.48	F
1.49	T
1.50	F
1.51	T
1.52	T
1.53	T
1.54	F
1.55	F
1.56	T
1.57	F

1.58	African, Protestant
1.59	Bible
1.60	vocal, clapping
1.61	North

1.62	T
1.63	T
1.64	F

1.65	F
1.66	F
1.67	T

1.68	Confederate
1.69	Virginia
1.70	Union
1.71	Ulysses S. Grant
1.72	graciously

1.73	anarchy
1.74	four
1.75	honor
1.76	revolution
1.77	defense

1.78	reading
1.79	law
1.80	Mary Todd
1.81	slavery
1.82	Stephen Douglas
1.83	forever
1.84	John Wilkes Booth
1.85	cemetery

1.86	equal
1.87	endure
1.88	live
1.89	perish

SECTION TWO

2.1	F		2.46	critic
2.2	T		2.47	ordinary
2.3	T		2.48	biography
2.4	F		2.49	editor
2.5	T		2.50	economic
2.6	F		2.51	realistic
2.7	F			
2.8	T		2.52	T
2.9	F		2.53	F
2.10	T		2.54	T
2.11	F		2.55	T
2.12	T		2.56	F
2.13	F		2.57	T
2.14	F		2.58	F
2.15	T		2.59	T
2.16	F		2.60	T
2.17	F		2.61	F
2.18	T		2.62	F
2.19	F		2.63	T
2.20	T		2.64	T
2.21	F		2.65	T
2.22	F		2.66	F
2.23	F		2.67	T
2.24	Lincoln		2.68	literary master
2.25	common		2.69	experience
2.26	Mississippi		2.70	William Dean Howells
2.27	steamboat		2.71	England
2.28	Mark Twain		2.72	point of view
2.29	speaker		2.73	narrative
2.30	Realism and Regionalism		2.74	character
2.31	pessimism			
2.32	religion		2.75	T
2.33	traditional		2.76	T
2.34	beginning		2.77	F
			2.78	T
2.35	T		2.79	T
2.36	T		2.80	T
2.37	F		2.81	T
2.38	T		2.82	F
2.39	F		2.83	F
2.40	F		2.84	T
2.41	T		2.85	F
2.42	T		2.86	T
2.43	F		2.87	T
2.44	T		2.88	F
2.45	T		2.89	T

SECTION THREE

3.1	naturalistic		3.38	T
3.2	Methodist		3.39	F
3.3	reporter		3.40	T
3.4	fame		3.41	T
3.5	newspaper		3.42	T
3.6	pessimism		3.43	F
3.7	accidental			

3.8	T		3.44	highest
3.9	F		3.45	poor
3.10	T		3.46	educate
3.11	F		3.47	Darwin
3.12	T		3.48	miner
3.13	T		3.49	evolutionary
3.14	F		3.50	popular, will
3.15	T			
3.16	F		3.51	F
3.17	T		3.52	T
3.18	T		3.53	T
3.19	F		3.54	T
			3.55	F
3.20	marriage		3.56	T
3.21	Louisiana		3.57	T
3.22	six		3.58	T
3.23	St. Louis		3.59	F
3.24	Louisiana		3.60	T
3.25	banned		3.61	T

3.26	Irony
3.27	heart
3.28	wept
3.29	joy
3.30	free
3.31	Brently Mallard
3.32	died

3.33	poet
3.34	slaves
3.35	Fredrick Douglas
3.36	black
3.37	novels

SECTION ONE

1.1	T
1.2	F
1.3	T
1.4	T
1.5	F
1.6	F
1.7	F
1.8	T
1.9	T
1.10	F
1.11	F
1.12	T
1.13	F
1.14	F
1.15	T
1.16	T
1.17	T
1.18	F
1.19	T
1.20	T
1.21	T
1.22	T
1.23	T
1.24	F
1.25	T
1.26	T
1.27	F
1.28	T
1.29	T
1.30	T
1.31	T
1.32	F
1.33	T
1.34	F
1.35	T

1.36	conservative
1.37	reporter
1.38	ambulance
1.39	Milan
1.40	Paris
1.41	clear
1.42	adjectives, nouns
1.43	truest
1.44	hunting, socializing
1.45	Spanish Civil War
1.46	depression

1.47	T
1.48	T
1.49	F
1.50	F
1.51	F
1.52	F
1.53	T
1.54	T
1.55	T
1.56	F
1.57	F

1.58	emptiness
1.59	Army
1.60	Zelda's
1.61	pleasure
1.62	mental
1.63	Hollywood, screenwriting
1.64	finished

1.65	T
1.66	T
1.67	F
1.68	T
1.69	T
1.70	F
1.71	T
1.72	F
1.73	F
1.74	T
1.75	T
1.76	F
1.77	T
1.78	T
1.79	T
1.80	F

SECTION TWO

2.1	traditional
2.2	Modernist
2.3	imagism
2.4	images
2.5	few
2.6	everyday
2.7	meaning
2.8	*The Cantos*
2.9	Italian
2.10	treason
2.11	insane

2.12	F
2.13	T
2.14	F
2.15	T
2.16	F

2.17	working
2.18	free
2.19	Chicago
2.20	four
2.21	Abraham Lincoln
2.22	*Complete Poems*
2.23	folk singer

2.24	F
2.25	F
2.26	T
2.27	F
2.28	T
2.29	T
2.30	T

2.31	experimental
2.32	traditional
2.33	past
2.34	detention
2.35	Paris, artist
2.36	freedom
2.37	immoral

2.38	F
2.39	T
2.40	T
2.41	F
2.42	T

2.43	poetry
2.44	regular full-time
2.45	first
2.46	imagination

2.47	dependent upon
2.48	Man
2.49	art, religion, believed
2.50	Pulitzer

2.51	T
2.52	T
2.53	F
2.54	F
2.55	T
2.56	F
2.57	T
2.58	F
2.59	T
2.60	T

2.61	Pulitzer Prizes
2.62	traditional, wise country
2.63	eleven
2.64	England
2.65	farm life
2.66	delight, wisdom
2.67	worldly
2.68	traditional, stay

2.69	T
2.70	F
2.71	T
2.72	T
2.73	F
2.74	T
2.75	T
2.76	F
2.77	T

2.78	traditional
2.79	English, Oxford
2.80	breakdown
2.81	individual
2.82	religion
2.83	*The Age of Anxiety*
2.84	satire

2.85	F
2.86	T
2.87	F
2.88	T
2.89	F
2.90	T
2.91	F
2.92	F
2.93	T
2.94	T

SECTION THREE

3.1	rhythm
3.2	mother
3.3	Columbia
3.4	world, seaman
3.5	plays, film scripts
3.6	hero
3.7	Los Angeles
3.8	cultural
3.9	American

3.10	T
3.11	F
3.12	T
3.13	F
3.14	T
3.15	T

3.16	playwright, novelist
3.17	Yale, Princeton
3.18	World War II
3.19	novel
3.20	*Our Town*
3.21	scenery, unconventional
3.22	reality
3.23	reproduced
3.24	traditional

3.25	F
3.26	F
3.27	T
3.28	T
3.29	F
3.30	T
3.31	F

3.32	F
3.33	T
3.34	T
3.35	F
3.36	T
3.37	F
3.38	T
3.39	F

3.40	inerrancy, fundamentalism's
3.41	Princeton
3.42	Christianity, liberal
3.43	modernists
3.44	secular intellectuals

3.45	T
3.46	F
3.47	T
3.48	T
3.49	F
3.50	T
3.51	F
3.52	F
3.53	T
3.54	T
3.55	F
3.56	T
3.57	F
3.58	T
3.59	F
3.60	F
3.61	T
3.62	T
3.63	T

SECTION ONE

1.1	technological
1.2	human reason
1.3	similar
1.4	truth
1.5	society
1.6	modern
1.7	human reason
1.8	Communism
1.9	oppression and brute force
1.10	communist
1.11	Thomas Paine
1.12	human reason
1.13	nature
1.14	animals
1.15	Christianity
1.16	50s
1.17	Space
1.18	technology
1.19	television
1.20	60s
1.21	John F. Kennedy
1.22	popular
1.23	Existentialism
1.24	always
1.25	Christian
1.26	God
1.27	God
1.28	morals
1.29	God
1.30	traditional
1.31	blurred
1.32	stream-of-consciousness
1.33	grotesque
1.34	man
1.35	grace
1.36	poetry
1.37	social
1.38	sinfulness
1.39	fatal
1.40	crippling
1.41	Christ
1.42	T
1.43	F
1.44	T
1.45	T

1.46	T
1.47	F
1.48	T
1.49	F
1.50	F
1.51	T
1.52	F
1.53	T
1.54	T
1.55	T
1.56	F
1.57	T
1.58	T
1.59	T
1.60	T
1.61	T
1.62	F
1.63	F
1.64	F
1.65	F
1.66	T
1.67	T
1.68	T
1.69	F
1.70	T
1.71	T
1.72	T
1.73	F
1.74	T
1.75	formless
1.76	traditional
1.77	greenhouses
1.78	childhood
1.79	peace
1.80	futile
1.81	ditch
1.82	light
1.83	snakes, yellow, necks
1.84	ripe, pulpy
1.85	nothing
1.86	breathing

SECTION TWO

2.1	fiction
2.2	photographer
2.3	South
2.4	novelist
2.5	Pulitzer
2.6	Mississippi

2.7	T
2.8	F
2.9	T
2.10	T
2.11	T
2.12	F
2.13	F
2.14	T
2.15	T
2.16	F
2.17	T
2.18	T
2.19	F
2.20	T
2.21	F
2.22	F
2.23	T

2.24	middle-class
2.25	social, cure
2.26	Pennsylvania

2.27	*The New Yorker*
2.28	television

2.29	T
2.30	F
2.31	F
2.32	T
2.33	F
2.34	F
2.35	T
2.36	T
2.37	F
2.38	F
2.39	T
2.40	T

2.41	change
2.42	New England
2.43	Harvard
2.44	traditional
2.45	confessional
2.46	plot, rhyme
2.47	lens
2.48	snapshot
2.49	dissatisfied
2.50	Vermeers
2.51	facts
2.52	living

SECTION THREE

3.1	Atlanta
3.2	Baptist
3.3	Boston
3.4	Mohandas K. Gandhi
3.5	boycott, segregation
3.6	Washington, protesters
3.7	biblical
3.8	Moses, Egypt

3.9	T
3.10	F
3.11	T
3.12	T
3.13	F
3.14	T
3.15	T
3.16	T
3.17	T
3.18	T
3.19	T

3.20	writer
3.21	Oklahoma
3.22	Harlem, trumpet
3.23	Langston Hughes
3.24	Americans
3.25	lectureships

3.26	T
3.27	T
3.28	F
3.29	F
3.30	F
3.31	T
3.32	T
3.33	F
3.34	T
3.35	F
3.36	T
3.37	T
3.38	T
3.39	T

3.40	Chicago
3.41	poetry
3.42	black
3.43	community, pride
3.44	traditional

3.45	T
3.46	F
3.47	F
3.48	T
3.49	F
3.50	T
3.51	F
3.52	T
3.53	T

TEST KEYS

SELF TEST 1

1.01	beliefs, thoughts
1.02	analyze, God
1.03	good
1.04	Bible
1.05	sovereignty
1.06	humble
1.07	Constitution
1.08	work
1.09	John Smith
1.010	Pocahontas
1.011	Native Americans
1.012	Indians (or Native Americans), Chickahominy
1.013	separatists
1.014	history, providential
1.015	a small
1.016	Separatists
1.017	Non-separatists
1.018	Christian
1.019	practicality
1.020	God's
1.021	Israelites
1.022	typology
1.023	the truth
1.024	creative
1.025	Indian-captivity narrative
1.026	American
1.027	Native Americans
1.028	Scriptures
1.029	Arbella
1.030	theocratic
1.031	F
1.032	T
1.033	T
1.034	T
1.035	F
1.036	F
1.037	T
1.038	T

For Thought and Discussion:

During the Pilgrims' first winter, over half of the company died because of poor housing, disease and starvation. At times, 2 or 3 people died each day. In all over 100 people died. Many of the stronger Pilgrims risked their lives to help those suffering from disease. As Christians, they put the needs of others above their own (Philippians 2:3-5). The crewmembers of the Mayflower suffered also from the harsh conditions. But in stark contrast to the Pilgrims, the crewmembers cursed one another and the Pilgrims, refusing to help one another.

Guide your student in a discussion of the differences between the Pilgrims and the crewmembers in the manner in which they faced adversity. Help your student to see that, in contrast to the world, the Christian's attitude in hard times should be one of contentment and trust (Philippians 4:10-13). The God who is sovereign never forgets His children (Luke 12:4-7).

SELF TEST 2

2.01   King Philip's
2.02   popular
2.03   sovereignty
2.04   God
2.05   change, actions

2.06   F
2.07   F
2.08   F
2.09   T
2.010 T
2.011 T
2.012 T
2.013 T
2.014 T
2.015 T
2.016 F
2.017 T

2.018 eight
2.019 brother-in-law
2.020 Church of England
2.021 minister
2.022 New England
2.023 toward; away from
2.024 business

For Thought and Discussion:

Bradstreet found comfort in God's sovereignty with the death of a grandchild. Like Job, she understood that the "Lord gives and the Lord takes away" (Job 1:21). Though she did not understand why God had allowed her grandchild to die, nevertheless, she trusted His wisdom in the situation. Similarly, Rowlandson found comfort in the fact that during all her troubles with the Native Americans that God was ultimately in control. She knew that not even a hair could fall from her head unless God had allowed it. And, when God did allow calamity to fall on her, then ultimately it would be for her good and His glory.

Guide your student in a discussion about God's sovereignty in the life of the believer. Help them to understand that "all things work to the good of those that love God, to those that are called according to His purpose" (Romans 8:28).

SELF TEST 3

3.01   F
3.02   T
3.03   F
3.04   F
3.05   T
3.06   F
3.07   T
3.08   F
3.09   T
3.010 T
3.011 T
3.012 F
3.013 T
3.014 T
3.015 T
3.016 T
3.017 T
3.018 T
3.019 F
3.020 F
3.021 T
3.022 F
3.023 T

3.024 America
3.025 Awakening
3.026 God's
3.027 human reason
3.028 protect, tyrannical
3.029 everything, nothing
3.030 God
3.031 life, death, grace, Christ
3.032 new, hands
3.033 mercy, sinners
3.034 self-made
3.035 self-improvement
3.036 advancement
3.037 center
3.038 influential
3.039 Britain
3.040 deist
3.041 church
3.042 stands, thanks
3.043 England
3.044 all, every
3.045 French
3.046 New York
3.047 citizen

For Thought and Discussion:

In his sermon, "Sinners in the Hands of an Angry God," Jonathan Edwards gives a striking message on the wrath of God and the mercy of God. His thesis is this: "There is nothing that keeps wicked men at any one moment out of hell, but the mere pleasure of God." The thesis is then underlined by ten points which explain man's position before God.

1. "There is no want of power in God to cast wicked men into hell at any moment."

2. "[The wicked] deserve to be cast into hell; so that divine justice never stands in the way, it makes no objection against God's using his power at any moment to destroy them."

3. "They are already under a sentence of condemnation to hell. They do not only justly deserve to be cast down thither, but the sentence of the law of God, that eternal and immutable rule of righteousness that God has fixed between him and mankind, is gone out against them, and stands against them; so that they are bound over already to hell. John iii. 18. "He that believeth not is condemned already."

4. "[The wicked] are now the objects of that very same anger and wrath of God, that is expressed in the torments of hell."

5. "The devil stands ready to fall upon them, and seize them as his own, at what moment God shall permit him. They belong to him; he has their souls in his possession, and under his dominion. The scripture represents them as his goods, Luke 11:12."

6. "There are in the souls of wicked men those hellish principles reigning, that would presently kindle and flame out into hell fire, if it were not for God's restraints."

7. "It is no security to wicked men for one moment, that there are no visible means of death at hand."

8. "Natural men's prudence and care to preserve their own lives, or the care of others to preserve them, do not secure them a moment."

9. "All wicked men's pains and contrivance which they use to escape hell, while they continue to reject Christ, and so remain wicked men, do not secure them from hell one moment."

10. "God has laid himself under no obligation, by any promise to keep any natural man out of hell one moment. God certainly has made no promises either of eternal life, or of any deliverance or preservation from eternal death, but what are contained in the covenant of grace, the promises that are given in Christ, in whom all the promises are yea and amen." Conclusively, Edwards pictures the sinner dangling over "hell's wide gapping mouth," held in safety only by God. Our own righteous works are but nothing to hold us up from the pit of hell. Urging his listeners to repent and turn to God in Christ, Edwards stresses that at any moment they might "plunge into the bottomless gulf" of hell. As a sinner, man can only find salvation in the redemptive work of Christ. He alone was able to endure the wrath of God on our behalf.

Guide your student in a discussion of man's sin, God's role in salvation, and religious works. Help him/her to understand that everyone is a sinner and therefore apart from Christ is under the just condemnation of God. Salvation cannot be found in good works (Job 15:14-16). God's wrath for our sin was satisfied in Christ. "Christ died for the ungodly . . . For if when we were enemies we were reconciled to God through the death of His Son, much more, having been reconciled, we shall be saved by His life" (Romans 5: 6, 10). This is the story of the Bible. God in His justice and mercy has saved His people from their sins. "That He might be just and the justifier of the one who has faith in Jesus" (Romans 3:26).

SELF TEST 1

1.01	T
1.02	F
1.03	F
1.04	T
1.05	F
1.06	T
1.07	F
1.08	T
1.09	F

1.010	novelist
1.011	hero
1.012	social

1.013	T
1.014	F
1.015	T
1.016	F

1.017	Catskill
1.018	henpecked
1.019	idleness
1.020	sleep
1.021	twenty
1.022	petticoat
1.023	writer
1.024	German
1.025	entertain
1.026	Romantic
1.027	women's rights, political
1.028	William Wordsworth

1.029	T
1.030	F
1.031	T

For Thought and Discussion:

Bryant believed that humans are just a part of nature and did not possess an eternal soul. When man dies he simply "becomes one" with the earth. In contrast, Hebrews 9:27 states that it is appointed for men once to die and then comes judgment. In other words, everyone will face the judgment of God one day. At the heart of Bryant's thinking is a denial of God. He did not believe that man will one day be held accountable for his sin. Because Bryant's belief system did not include the reality of sin, it also denied the need for a Savior. If man is not bound to face judgment for his sins, then there is no need for a Savior.

Guide your student in a discussion of Bryant's belief system. Help him to understand that it denies the truth of God's coming judgment and salvation in Christ for the believer.

SELF TEST 2

2.01 F
2.02 T
2.03 F
2.04 T
2.05 F
2.06 F
2.07 T
2.08 T
2.09 T
2.010 F

2.011 poetry
2.012 rhythms
2.013 optimistic
2.014 Quaker, abolitionist
2.015 Christian love
2.016 farm
2.017 amazement
2.018 solitude
2.019 secure
2.020 medicine
2.021 novels
2.022 dinner speaker
2.023 Romantic
2.024 sinfulness, Jesus
2.025 Unitarian
2.026 traditional
2.027 Thoreau and Whitman
2.028 sublime
2.029 heart
2.030 heroes', foe
2.031 wave
2.032 self-reliance
2.033 institutions
2.034 Walden Pond, transcendental
2.035 resist
2.036 himself
2.037 free verse
2.038 rhyme
2.039 shift

2.040 T
2.041 F
2.042 F
2.043 T
2.044 F
2.045 F
2.046 T
2.047 T
2.048 T

For Thought and Discussion:

Ralph Waldo Emerson believed that man was essentially good. Sin and corruption came from social institutions and not from the heart of man. The universe was god, and god was the universe. In a sense, he was a pantheist. Man, therefore as part of the universe, was as Emerson put it, "part or parcel of God." Since evil came from society, Nature was looked to as a moral guide. It was in a sense the "scriptures" of the transcendentalists. They exalted its virtues as divine. But since Nature does not have a definite moral code, there existed many contradictions among transcendental beliefs. Transcendentalists were in fact looking to themselves for answers, formulating whatever set morals they felt comfortable with. As Emerson said of his moral guide, "I deemed I was thinking justly or doing right."

In light of Romans 1:18-32, the transcendentalists "exchanged the truth of God for a lie" at many points. At the core of their rejection of the truth of God was their pantheistic belief that god is in and part of the universe. Their exaltation of Nature as a moral guide is tantamount to worshipping the creation as if it were the Creator. Consequently, a universal standard of morals is removed. Man is left alone to decide "what is truth." Moral relativity sets in with the rejection of the God of the Bible.

Guide your student in a discussion of the differences between transcendentalism and Biblical truth. Help the student to understand that the Bible is given to us by God and is our rule for truth, life and godliness (2 Timothy 3:16).

SELF TEST 3

3.01   guilt
3.02   Puritan
3.03   guilt
3.04   frustration
3.05   decline
3.06   Hawthorne
3.07   1920s

3.08   T
3.09   T
3.010 F
3.011 T
3.012 T

3.013 Lenore
3.014 window, Pallas
3.015 nevermore
3.016 Aidenn
3.017 two
3.018 Philadelphia
3.019 success
3.020 single
3.021 Horror, melancholy

3.022 T
3.023 F
3.024 T
3.025 T
3.026 T
3.027 T
3.028 T

3.029 untraditional
3.030 seven
3.031 Amherst
3.032 happiness, world

3.033 F
3.034 F
3.035 F
3.036 F
3.037 F

For Thought and Discussion:

In Melville's chapter of *Moby Dick*, "The Whiteness of the Whale," there are listed various examples from past cultures and religions of the fearsomeness of white. Throughout history the color white has been used as a symbol of purity, reverence and power. Interestingly enough, it has always and everywhere caused fear in the heart of man.

Guide your student in a discussion of the relationship between God's holiness and the purity of white. After discussing Melville's examples from pagan religions and his note that "white is the very veil of the Christian Deity," read Isaiah 6:1-5 aloud to your student. Point out Isaiah's reaction to God's presence was one of fear and reverence. Isaiah reacted this way because the sight of God's holiness reminded him of his comparable sinfulness (v. 5) and just condemnation before a holy God. God's holiness is communicated to us in the appearance of white. Jesus during his transfiguration was described to have been clothed in a gleaming white robe. White has not a hint of impurity. Thus, the appearance of white anywhere should remind our conscience that we are sinful, and apart from the grace of God in Jesus are under fearful condemnation.

SELF TEST 1

1.01	T
1.02	F
1.03	F
1.04	F
1.05	F
1.06	T
1.07	T
1.08	T
1.09	F
1.010	F
1.011	T
1.012	T
1.013	F

1.014	read, write
1.015	Union
1.016	discriminated
1.017	African, Protestant
1.018	Bible
1.019	North
1.020	Confederate
1.021	Virginia
1.022	graciously
1.023	reading
1.024	forever
1.025	John Wilkes Booth

1.026	T
1.027	F
1.028	T
1.029	T
1.030	F
1.031	T
1.032	F
1.033	T
1.034	T
1.035	T
1.036	F
1.037	T

1.038	Abraham Lincoln
1.039	most
1.040	500,000
1.041	revolution
1.042	defense
1.043	perish

For Thought and Discussion:

In *My Freedom and My Bondage*, Fredrick Douglass describes the cruelty that he suffered as a boy and as a young man. While a boy, he is forbidden to read and write because his master feared that it would increase his desire for freedom. As a young man, he is stripped of his daily wages and beaten like an animal in order to break his spirit. In Harriet Beecher Stowe's novel, *Uncle Tom's Cabin*, Tom is beaten needlessly to the point of death. Yet Tom, as a Christian, finds hope and peace in God. He is able to endure his sufferings because His Lord also endured as a silent Lamb before His butchers. Cassey, on the other hand, is unable to have Tom's attitude. She is a woman who has suffered the loss of children and dignity at the hand of cruel masters. As an unbeliever, she cannot see that God is in control of all things, even the terrible things. Because of her suffering she doubts the existence of God.

Guide your student in a discussion of slavery in American before the Civil War. Help the student to imagine what it would be like to lose your freedom and be enslaved to a cruel master. Also, help them to understand the incompatibility of the type of slavery that existed in America and Christianity. (The slavery that existed in ancient Israel was not a livelong or an oppressive slavery. A slave was in a sense an indentured servant or bondservant that was eventually freed. Cruelty and oppression towards slaves was forbidden according to Deuteronomy 15:12-18).

SELF TEST 2

2.01	T
2.02	T
2.03	T
2.04	F
2.05	T
2.06	T
2.07	F
2.08	T
2.09	F
2.010	T
2.011	F
2.012	T
2.013	F
2.014	T
2.015	F
2.016	most
2.017	perish
2.018	common
2.019	Realism and Regionalism
2.020	beginning
2.021	literary master
2.022	point-of-view
2.023	narrative
2.024	F
2.025	F
2.026	T
2.027	F
2.028	T
2.029	T
2.030	T
2.031	F
2.032	T
2.033	F
2.034	T
2.035	T
2.036	read, write
2.037	African, Protestant
2.038	forever
2.039	graciously
2.040	critic
2.041	ordinary

For Thought and Discussion:

Huck has been taught by southern society that a white man has the right to own a black man. Because slavery has been endorsed by both church ministers and other authority figures, Huck is convinced that he would be acting "righteous" if he returns his friend Jim back to slavery. But Huck decides to return to "wickedness" and help Jim remain free. Rightly so, Huck's conscience is described as "deformed." The society that he lives in has put undue guilt upon him. Consequently, Huck is skeptical of the church and its practices. According to their "doctrines" he is doomed for hell.

Guide your student in a discussion of the effects of society on a person's conscience. Help the student to understand that many times society will "teach the doctrines of men as the commands of God" (Mark 7:7). Just because something is legal does not make it right (e.g. abortion). As Christians, the Bible must be our only rule of life and godliness. It alone must guide our consciences. The slavery that existed in the South prior to the Civil War did much to harm the preaching of the gospel. Because so called Christians, practiced a cruel and oppressive form of slavery, men like Mark Twain were led to say, "there is no God . . . no heaven, no hell."

SELF TEST 3

3.01 ordinary
3.02 African, Protestant
3.03 forever
3.04 read, write
3.05 naturalistic
3.06 reporter
3.07 fame
3.08 accidental
3.09 heart
3.010 joy
3.011 died

3.012 T
3.013 T
3.014 F
3.015 F
3.016 F
3.017 T
3.018 F
3.019 T
3.020 T
3.021 T
3.022 T
3.023 T
3.024 F
3.025 T
3.026 T
3.027 T
3.028 F
3.029 T
3.030 F
3.031 T
3.032 T
3.033 T

3.034 most
3.035 perish
3.036 Realism and Regionalism
3.037 point-of-view
3.038 marriage
3.039 Louisiana
3.040 banned
3.041 poet
3.042 black
3.043 highest
3.044 evolutionary
3.045 popular, will

For Thought and Discussion:

As an evolutionist, Jack London believed that the "law of life" was death. Weaker animals must die in order for the stronger ones to live. London thought humans were nothing more than animals and therefore subject to the "law of life." In his short story, "The Law of Life," London pictures the death of an elderly Inuit man. The weak old man is left behind to die in the snow as the tribe moves on to look for food. His death is a "needful" one that will help the tribe survive. In the face of death, the old man tries to console his fears with the "law of life." The story leaves one with animalistic view of man and an amoral view of the universe.

Guide your student in a discussion of the differences between London's belief and the Bible. Help the student to understand that London's view of man does not agree with the Biblical view of man. Man is made in the image of God, and therefore is not like the animals but has dominion over them. Like his God, man possesses dignity, intelligence and a will. He also possesses a spirit and is therefore morally responsible for his actions. As Christians, we are called to obey the Law of God rather than the "law of life." The Law of God is summed up in a love for God and a love for others (Matthew 22:37-40). As opposed to a self-centered, animalistic sense of survival, love and self-sacrifice is to be our overriding attitude (Philippians 2:3-4). The more the Holy Spirit enables a Christian to adhere to the Law of God, the more God's moral image is reflected in his life. And thus, he behaves not like the animalistic Inuit of London's story, but like the human God created him to be (Colossians 3:10).

SELF TEST 1

1.01	F
1.02	F
1.03	F
1.04	F
1.05	T
1.06	F
1.07	F
1.08	F
1.09	F
1.010	T
1.011	T
1.012	T
1.013	T
1.014	T
1.015	T
1.016	T
1.017	T
1.018	F

1.019	conservative
1.020	Paris
1.021	clear
1.022	adjectives, nouns
1.023	hunting, socializing
1.024	depression
1.025	emptiness
1.026	Zelda's
1.027	mental
1.028	Hollywood, screenwriting

1.029	T
1.030	T
1.031	F
1.032	T
1.033	T
1.034	T
1.035	T
1.036	T

1.037	modernist
1.038	compresses
1.039	interpretation
1.040	jazz and blues
1.041	black

For Thought and Discussion:

From an early age, Dexter Green finds "glittering thing" desirous. Judy Jones is one of those "glittering things." Like the woman of Proverbs 5 & 7, she is "loud and rebellious." Her speech is "smoother than oil" and she promises "peace offerings" to those she kisses. It is not long after Dexter begins a relationship with Judy that he discovers that he is only one of her many lovers or rather "victims she has cast down." But despite her "crafty heart," Dexter continues to admire her and want her. So possessed with his desire for her, he even risks his engagement to a nice young lady to have another chance to be with Judy. At the end of the story, Dexter hears news of Judy's marriage to another man. A friend reports that she is no longer attractive. Dexter becomes disillusioned. His "glittering things" have failed to fulfill their promises of happiness. Dexter feels dead inside. Those things that he had longed for have only left him empty and alone.

Guide your student in a discussion of the deceitfulness of lust in the modern age. Help the student to understand how Judy, like the harlot of Proverbs 7, led Dexter down to the "chambers of death." Sin not only leads to death in the eternal sense but it also leads to a death that we endure while on earth (James 1:14-15). Sin brings destruction to our lives. Like many of the modern age, Dexter felt empty and alone because he had pursued a lustful appetite and wanted those things that God has forbidden. His relationship with a wicked woman did not lead to peace and happiness but to pain and loneliness. Judy's house was "the way to hell" for Dexter, spiritually and emotionally. Like a dumb ox, she led him to "the slaughter."

SELF TEST 2

2.01	compresses
2.02	interpretation
2.03	jazz and blues
2.04	traditional
2.05	Modernist
2.06	imagism
2.07	images
2.08	few
2.09	insane
2.010	working
2.011	free
2.012	experimental
2.013	traditional
2.014	past
2.015	poetry
2.016	dependent upon
2.017	Man
2.018	traditional, wise country
2.019	farm life
2.020	delight, wisdom
2.021	T
2.022	T
2.023	T
2.024	T
2.025	F
2.026	T
2.027	F
2.028	T
2.029	F
2.030	T
2.031	T
2.032	T
2.033	F
2.034	T
2.035	F
2.036	T
2.037	T
2.038	clear
2.039	emptiness
2.040	traditional
2.041	religion
2.042	satire

For Thought and Discussion:

Many modern artists and writers suffered from bouts of depression and/or anxiety. Ernest Hemingway was hospitalized throughout his career for depression. Eventually he killed himself. Ezra Pound was deemed insane and kept at St. Elizabeth's hospital after his trial for treason. It is obvious that the modern world with its "adultery, fornication, uncleanness, lewdness, idolatry, sorcery, hatred, contentions, jealousies, outbursts of wrath, selfish ambitions, dissensions, heresies, envy, murders, drunkenness, revelries, and the like" did not lead these men to "love, joy, peace, longsuffering, kindness, goodness, meekness, faithfulness, gentleness, self-control" (Galatians 5:19-23).

Guide your student in a discussion of the works of the flesh and the fruit of the Spirit as evidenced in the lives of unbelievers and believers. People are either saved or unsaved. Consequently, they are either consumed by the "fire of the Holy Spirit" or the "fires of the flesh." Sin or "fires of the flesh" cause great despair because their temporary pleasures promise peace and happiness but never deliver; lust is deceitful. Lasting hope and happiness can only come from being "consumed by the fire of the Holy Spirit" (Galatians 5:22-23). A life of faith and holiness makes one joyful, peaceful and kind.

SELF TEST 3

3.01   clear
3.02   emptiness
3.03   religion
3.04   satire
3.05   rhythm
3.06   hero
3.07   cultural
3.08   American
3.09   playwright, novelist
3.010   scenery, unconventional
3.011   reality

3.012   T
3.013   T
3.014   T
3.015   T
3.016   T
3.017   F
3.018   T
3.019   T
3.020   F
3.021   T
3.022   T
3.023   F
3.024   F
3.025   T
3.026   T
3.027   T
3.028   T
3.029   F
3.030   F
3.031   T
3.032   F
3.033   F
3.034   F
3.035   T
3.036   T
3.037   T
3.038   F
3.039   T
3.040   T

3.041   compresses
3.042   interpretation
3.043   jazz and blues
3.044   traditional
3.045   imagism
3.046   images
3.047   working
3.048   experimental
3.049   poetry
3.050   delight, wisdom
3.051   inerrancy, fundamentalism's
3.052   Christianity, liberal
3.053   modernists

For Thought and Discussion:

As the church entered the modern era, many Protestants wanted to accommodate religion to the scientific and social movements of the age. In opposition to liberal Protestants (modernists), Fundamentalists insisted upon the historical truthfulness of the Bible and the occurrence of supernatural events. At the heart of the controversy was the Bible. Liberals denied it to be the complete and accurate Word of God. Fundamentalists affirmed its inerrancy. J. Gresham Machen was a champion of fundamentalism. His book, *Christianity and Liberalism*, identified liberalism as a new religion because of its views of God, man and the way of salvation, strayed so far from those laid out in Scripture. Liberalism's view of man is an optimistic one. Liberalism does not have a concept of sin. It believes that man has the ability to "save" himself by being like Christ, or rather by living according to the law. It is another form of legalism. Christianity views man as sinful and hopelessly lost apart from Christ. Christianity deals with sin squarely. Men are saved by grace through faith alone. The Bible to the Christian is his only rule of faith and life. It is without error and complete. Liberalism sees the Bible as just another religious book among many. It contains truth, but the supernatural events that it records are only myths. In the Liberal view, the resurrection of Jesus, Jonah's experience in the whale and other miracles did not really happen. Because liberal Protestantism has denied the inerrancy and authority of Scripture, they have contributed to the moral relativity that now exists in American society. They have replaced the Word of God with the opinion of men.

Guide your student in a discussion of the importance of the Bible to the Christian faith. Help the student to understand that the Bible is "an account of a revelation from God to man, which is found nowhere else" [It] concerns the way by which sinful man can come into communion with the living God" (Romans 15:4; 2 Timothy 3:16; 2 Peter 1:21). It is also a "narration of [the death and resurrection of Christ]." Without that event, the world "is altogether dark, and humanity is lost under the guilt of sin" (1 Corinthians 15:17). In other words, Christianity is utterly dependent upon the accuracy and truthfulness of the Word of God. The Scriptures are the Christian's only rule to faith and life.

SELF TEST 1

1.01	modern
1.02	human reason
1.03	Communism
1.04	communist
1.05	Christianity
1.06	50s
1.07	technology
1.08	television
1.09	60s
1.010	popular
1.011	Existentialism
1.012	always
1.013	Christian
1.014	God
1.015	sinfulness
1.016	Christ
1.017	similar
1.018	universal
1.019	society
1.020	morals
1.021	God
1.022	traditional
1.023	blurred
1.024	stream-of-consciousness
1.025	grotesque
1.026	poetry
1.027	social
1.028	formless
1.029	valued
1.030	childhood
1.031	peace
1.032	futile
1.033	nothing
1.034	breathing
1.035	F
1.036	T
1.037	F
1.038	T
1.039	T
1.040	F
1.041	F
1.042	T
1.043	T
1.044	F
1.045	T
1.046	T
1.047	F
1.048	T

For Thought and Discussion:

Flannery O'Connor's short story, "The Displaced Person," has six main characters: the priest, Mr. Guizac, Mrs. McIntyre, Mr. & Mrs. Shortley, and the elderly black man. The priest is a kind, caring minister that only wishes to help the Guizacs and Mrs. McIntyre. He is likened unto one that brings the gospel to a sinful people. Mr. Guizac, also called the "Displaced Person," is a foreign refuge from Eastern Europe who has been brought with his family to Mrs. McIntyre farm by the priest. Mr. Guizac is also a hard worker that does not complain about his wages nor about the laziness of the other workers. He is likened unto Jesus Christ. Mrs. McIntyre is a stingy widow who believes herself to be the poorest woman in the world. She expects everyone to work hard for her but does not want to give much in return. She loves Mr. Guizac's hard work until the priest tells her that she is morally responsible for him. Mrs. Shortley thinks she is a good Christian, yet she is an incessant gossip and a slanderer. From the moment she sets eyes on Mr. Guizac she believes him to be from the devil and attempts to convince Mrs. McIntyre of her idea. Mr. Shortley is no better than his wife. He is lazy, yet complains to Mrs. McIntyre about Mr. Guizac. Blaming Mr. Guizac for his wife's death, Mr. Shortley allows a tracker to roll over and kill him. Discuss with your student how the language used by some of the characters is sinful and not to be used today. The tone and language that shows inequality and disrespect connects to the characterization.

After reading 1 John 3:7-18, guide your student in a discussion of the characters and their spiritual condition and seek to love the people that hate them. Mr. Guizac and the priest possess the characteristics of the children of God. They practice righteousness. On the other hand, Mrs. McIntyre and the Shortleys resemble the children of the devil. They practice sin and hate Mr. Guizac. In fact, their hatred is so strong towards him, they eventually kill him or allow him to be killed. Like Cain who murdered his brother, and the Jews that murdered their Christ, Mrs. McIntyre and the Shortleys murder Mr. Guizac because their works were evil and his righteous.

SELF TEST 2

2.01	truth
2.02	traditional
2.03	God
2.04	valued
2.05	lose
2.06	middle-class
2.07	social, cure
2.08	television
2.09	plot, rhyme
2.010	lens

2.011	T
2.012	T
2.013	T
2.014	F
2.015	T
2.016	F
2.017	F
2.018	T
2.019	F
2.020	F
2.021	T
2.022	T
2.023	T
2.024	T

2.025	fiction
2.026	South
2.027	Mississippi
2.028	human reason
2.029	Christianity
2.030	Existentialism
2.031	God
2.032	sinfulness
2.033	communist
2.034	change
2.035	New England
2.036	traditional
2.037	confessional
2.038	snapshot
2.039	facts
2.040	living

For Thought and Discussion:

John Updike's short story "Separating" portrays a modern American couple who have decided to separate, even though they "get along." The story focuses on how the parents plan to tell their teen and young adult children that their father is leaving the next day, and how the revelation is actually made. The plot centers on the mental and emotional strug-

gles of Richard, the father, who wrestles with growing regret and doubt over the decision, leading to a crisis when confronting his eldest son's agonized question—Why? In this cathartic moment, Richard appears to give over to a sense that the separation has no legitimate purpose. As a striking contrast, Joan, his wife, remains cool, calm, and convinced that separation (and possibly divorce) is the only course remaining.

Note: Many of your students will have been impacted by divorce, either in their own homes or extended families. Be sensitive as students work through Updike's short story "Separating" and the discussion assignment, permitting them to express their own emotional responses without probing into their personal experiences.

Guide your student in a discussion of the validity of Richard and Joan's separation based upon Matthew 19:8-9. Encourage the student to explore the context of the larger passage beginning at verse 3. The Scripture passage indicates that divorce is not God's plan, but is permitted under certain clearly defined and very narrow circumstances. In the words of Jesus: "Moses because of the hardness of your hearts suffered you to put away your wives: but from the beginning it was not so. And I say unto you, Whosoever shall put away his wife, except it be for fornication, and shall marry another, committeth adultery: and whoso marrieth her which is put away doth commit adultery" (KJV). Encourage the student to evaluate the parents' decision to separate against this clear Biblical standard. Make sure the student supports considerations and conclusions with relevant details from the story and from the Scripture passage.

Some discerning student readers may note that the parents' explanation to their children does not appear to be the full story. It could be argued that Joan's statement that "they liked each other but did not make each other happy enough, somehow" may be undermined by Richard's statement to Joan in private: "...they never questioned the reasons we gave. No thought of a third person." Thus, some students may argue that infidelity may be the root cause of the separation, affecting their evaluation in light of the Biblical standard. All students should observe that the parents appear willing to pursue their own preferences for "freedom," despite the impact that a possible divorce could have on the children, perhaps illustrating the kind of "hardness of heart" Jesus refers to in Matthew.

SELF TEST 3

3.01	truth
3.02	lose
3.03	valued
3.04	middle-class
3.05	social
3.06	Baptist
3.07	Mohandas K. Gandhi
3.08	Washington, protestors
3.09	Moses, Egypt
3.010	poetry
3.011	black
3.012	community, pride
3.013	traditional

3.014	T
3.015	T
3.016	T
3.017	T
3.018	T
3.019	T
3.020	T
3.021	T
3.022	T
3.023	F
3.024	T
3.025	T
3.026	T
3.027	T
3.028	F
3.029	T
3.030	T

3.031	Christianity
3.032	change
3.033	sinfulness
3.034	writer
3.035	Harlem, trumpet
3.036	Langston Hughes
3.037	Americans

For Thought and Discussion:

Dr. Martin Luther King, Jr. led a March on Washington in August of 1963. The purpose of the speech was to bring to the attention of the nation that according to the governing documents of the United States and the Christian concept of brotherhood that "all men are created equal." Thus, black people and other minorities deserve the same freedoms as other men.

In light of Colossians 3:11, "there is neither Greek nor Jew, circumcised nor uncircumcised, barbarian, Scythian, slave nor free, but Christ is all and in all," lead your student in a discussion of the connection between Christianity and the equality of all men. The concept of the equality of all men/women has played an important part in the Civil Rights movement because it is based upon Scripture. If you are a Christian, you cannot deny its truth. Dr. Martin Luther King's use of the Christian concept of brotherhood is only a continuation of the tie between religion and freedom that has been an integral part of the nation since its inception. In the early 1800s, Alexis de Tocqueville observed that in the United States, freedom is "intimately united" to religion. Later on, during the Second Great Awakening, revivalists often called for the abolition of slavery on the grounds of Christian love and the equality of all men. And in our own day, ministers are still found at the forefront of the Civil Rights movement.

1. Scripture
2. Bible
3. Puritan
4. Virginia
5. history
6. sufferings
7. God
8. glorify
9. T
10. T
11. F
12. F
13. T
14. T
15. F
16. brother-in-law
17. Church of England
18. minister
19. New England
20. materialism
21. F
22. T
23. F
24. F
25. T
26. F
27. F
28. T
29. F
30. F
31. F
32. T
33. F

34. small
35. practicality
36. God's
37. Israelites
38. truth
39. Indian-captivity narrative
40. *Arbella*
41. theocratic
42. God
43. grace
44. angry
45. advancement
46. man, God
47. writer
48. thanks
49. French
50. America
51. God's
52. human reason
53. nothing

Thinking and Writing:

Whichever topic is chosen, look for important facts and points that were discussed with the student during the corresponding "For Thought and Discussion" exercise. The paper should communicate the subject matter in a clear, organized manner. Correct grammar and punctuation should be used.

1.	F	41.	resist
2.	F	42.	free verse
3.	T	43.	rhyme
4.	F	44.	American
5.	F	45.	T
6.	F	46.	F
7.	F	47.	T
8.	Catskill	48.	T
9.	henpecked	49.	F
10.	20	50.	guilt
11.	happy	51.	Puritan
12.	writer	52.	frustration
13.	German	53.	Hawthorne
14.	Romantic	54.	1920s
15.	William Wordsworth	55.	Lenore
16.	T	56.	nevermore
17.	F	57.	heaven
18.	F	58.	Philadelphia
19.	T	59.	single
20.	T	60.	Horror, melancholy
21.	F	61.	untraditional
22.	F	62.	seven
23.	T	63.	happiness, bitterness
24.	novelist	64.	F
25.	hero	65.	F
26.	poetry	66.	F
27.	rhythms	67.	F
28.	Quaker, abolitionist	68.	F
29.	farm	69.	T
30.	amazement	70.	F
31.	medicine	71.	T
32.	dinner speaker	72.	T
33.	Romantic	73.	T
34.	sinfulness, Jesus		
35.	Unitarian		
36.	Thoreau		
37.	sublime		
38.	wave		
39.	institutions		
40.	Walden Pond, transcendental		

Thinking and Writing:

Whichever topic is chosen, look for important facts and points that were discussed with the student during the corresponding "For Thought and Discussion" exercise. The paper should communicate the subject matter in a clear, organized manner. Correct grammar and punctuation should be used.

1. read
2. free
3. ordinary
4. naturalistic
5. meaningless
6. died
7. defeat
8. North
9. musical
10. novels
11. revolution
12. government
13. colloquial
14. Henry James
15. women
16. Louisiana
17. black
18. traditional
19. writers
20. evolutionary
21. F
22. T
23. F

24. F
25. F
26. F
27. F
28. T
29. T
30. F
31. F
32. T
33. F
34. T
35. F
36. F
37. T
38. F
39. F
40. F

Thinking and Writing:

Whichever topic is chosen, look for important facts and points that were discussed with the student during the corresponding "For Thought and Discussion" exercise. The paper should communicate the subject matter in a clear, organized manner. Correct grammar and punctuation should be used.

1.	clear and precise	29.	F
2.	adjectives	30.	F
3.	emptiness	31.	F
4.	religion	32.	T
5.	satire	33.	F
6.	Langston Hughes	34.	compresses
7.	black	35.	interpretation
8.	American	36.	jazz and blues
9.	Wilder's	37.	traditional
10.	F	38.	Modernist
11.	F	39.	imagism
12.	F	40.	images
13.	F	41.	working
14.	T	42.	free
15.	F	43.	familiar
16.	F	44.	poetry
17.	F	45.	man
18.	F	46.	delight, wisdom
19.	F	47.	farm life
20.	T	48.	inerrancy, fundamentalism's
21.	F	49.	modernists
22.	F		
23.	T		
24.	F		
25.	F		
26.	T		
27.	T		
28.	T		

Thinking and Writing:

Whichever topic is chosen, look for important facts and points that were discussed with the student during the corresponding "For Thought and Discussion" exercise. The paper should communicate the subject matter in a clear, organized manner. Correct grammar and punctuation should be used.

1. truth
2. lose
3. grotesque
4. postmodern
5. stream-of-consciousness
6. valued
7. social
8. peace
9. breathing
10. middle
11. societal
12. Gandhi
13. Moses, Egypt
14. poetry
15. pride
16. traditional
17. poetry
18. F
19. F
20. F
21. T
22. F
23. F
24. T
25. F
26. F

27. F
28. F
29. F
30. T
31. F
32. South
33. Christianity
34. human reason
35. Existentialism
36. God
37. television
38. Christian
39. modern
40. change
41. sinfulness
42. snapshot
43. facts
44. writer
45. Americans

Thinking and Writing:

Whichever topic is chosen, look for important facts and points that were discussed with the student during the corresponding "For Thought and Discussion" exercise. The paper should communicate the subject matter in a clear, organized manner. Correct grammar and punctuation should be used.

1. analyze, God
2. Bible
3. sovereignty
4. Pocahontas
5. history, providential
6. King Philip's
7. God
8. change, actions
9. F
10. T
11. T
12. T
13. T
14. T
15. F
16. brother-in-law
17. Church of England
18. minister
19. New England
20. toward, away from
21. F
22. F
23. T
24. T
25. T
26. F
27. T
28. T
29. F
30. F
31. T
32. T
33. F
34. F

35. a small
36. practicality
37. God's
38. Israelites
39. the truth
40. Indian-captivity narrative
41. Arbella
42. theocratic
43. God
44. life, grace
45. hands
46. advancement
47. center
48. influential
49. stands
50. French
51. America
52. God's
53. human reason
54. everything, nothing

1.	T	38.	sublime
2.	T	39.	wave
3.	T	40.	institutions
4.	F	41.	Walden Pond, transcendental
5.	T	42.	resist
6.	T	43.	free verse
7.	T	44.	rhyme
8.	T	45.	shift
9.	Catskill	46.	T
10.	henpecked	47.	T
11.	twenty	48.	F
12.	petticoat	49.	F
13.	writer	50.	T
14.	German	51.	guilt
15.	Romantic	52.	Puritan
16.	William Wordsworth	53.	frustration
17.	F	54.	Hawthorne
18.	T	55.	1920s
19.	T	56.	Lenore
20.	F	57.	nevermore
21.	F	58.	Aidenn
22.	T	59.	Philadelphia
23.	T	60.	single
24.	F	61.	Horror, melancholy
25.	novelist	62.	untraditional
26.	hero	63.	seven
27.	poetry	64.	happiness, world
28.	rhythm	65.	T
29.	Quaker, abolitionist	66.	T
30.	farm	67.	T
31.	amazement	68.	T
32.	medicine	69.	T
33.	dinner speaker	70.	T
34.	Romantic	71.	T
35.	sinfulness, Jesus	72.	F
36.	Unitarian	73.	F
37.	Thoreau and Whitman	74.	F

1.	William Dean Howells	21.	T
2.	musical, hymns	22.	F
3.	free	23.	F
4.	Fredrick Douglass's	24.	T
5.	Stephen Crane	25.	F
6.	meaningless	26.	T
7.	dies	27.	T
8.	southerners	28.	T
9.	North	29.	F
10.	novels	30.	F
11.	revolution	31.	T
12.	government	32.	F
13.	colloquial	33.	F
14.	Henry James	34.	F
15.	women	35.	F
16.	Louisiana	36.	T
17.	black	37.	F
18.	traditional	38.	T
19.	writers	39.	T
20.	evolutionary	40.	F

1.	clear	28.	F
2.	adjectives	29.	F
3.	emptiness	30.	T
4.	religion	31.	T
5.	satire	32.	T
6.	rhythm	33.	F
7.	cultural	34.	T
8.	American	35.	compresses
9.	scenery, unconventional	36.	interpretation
10.	reality	37.	jazz and blues
11.	T	38.	traditional
12.	T	39.	Modernist
13	T	40.	imagism
14.	T	41.	images
15.	T	42.	working
16.	T	43.	free
17.	T	44.	experimental
18.	T	45.	poetry
19.	T	46.	man
20.	T	47.	delight, wisdom
21.	F	48.	farm life
22.	T	49.	inerrancy, fundamentalism's
23.	F	50.	modernists
24.	F		
25.	T		
26.	T		
27.	T		

1.	truth	24.	T
2.	lose	25.	T
3.	grotesque	26.	T
4.	postmodern	27.	T
5.	stream-of-consciousness	28.	T
6.	valued	29.	T
7.	social	30.	F
8.	peace	31.	T
9.	breathing	32.	South
10.	middle-class	33.	Christianity
11.	societal	34.	human reason
12.	Gandhi	35.	Existentialism
13.	Moses, Egypt	36.	God
14.	Brooks'	37.	television
15.	community, pride	38.	Christian
16.	traditional	39.	modern
17.	poetry	40.	change
18.	T	41.	sinfulness
19.	T	42.	snapshot
20.	T	43.	facts
21.	F	44.	writer
22.	T	45.	Americans
23.	T		